Assessment Clear and Simple

Jossey-Bass Higher Education Series

Assessment Clear and Simple

A Practical Guide for Institutions, Departments, and General Education

Second Edition

Barbara E. Walvoord
Foreword by Trudy W. Banta

JOSSEY-BASS
A Wiley Imprint
www.josseybass.com

Published by Jossey-Bass
A Wiley Imprint
989 Market Street, San Francisco, CA 94103-1741—www.josseybass.com

Library of Congress Cataloging-in-Publication Data

Walvoord, Barbara E. Fassler, 1941-
    Assessment clear and simple : a practical guide for institutions, departments, and general education/Barbara E. Walvoord; foreword by Trudy W. Banta.—2nd ed.

        p. cm.
    Includes bibliographical references and index.
    ISBN 978-0-470-54119-7 (pbk.)
        1.   Educational evaluation. I. Title.
    LB2822.75W35 2010
    379.1'58—dc22

2009049497

Printed in the United States of America

SECOND EDITION

PB Printing   10 9 8 7 6 5 4 3 2 1

Contents

To the wonderful people at more than 350 institutions where I have consulted and led workshops—people who have been generous hosts in every way, who have not only listened but also shared their own creative insights and practices, and who have not only sought to learn from my experience but also taught me, challenged me, made me think, and provided me with the examples that fill this book

Foreword to the First Edition

IN OUR RESPECTIVE travels around the country talking with faculty about assessment, Barbara Walvoord and I have heard this question many times: "How do we get started in assessment?" That is often followed with a plea, "Isn't there a simple step-by-step guide we can follow?" Until this point, we have had to say no to that entreaty. But now Barbara has stepped forward to present *Assessment Clear and Simple,* and all of us—the novices who seek help and experienced practitioners who try to provide it—are indebted to her.

In clear, persuasive prose that reflects her grounding in the discipline of English, Barbara brings us a straightforward definition of assessment that emphasizes the use of carefully considered evidence to improve learning. True to her promise in the subtitle to keep her message short, Barbara defines her audience narrowly and then tells each of three groups that they need to read just two of the book's four chapters! There is an introductory chapter for everyone, then a special chapter each for institution-wide planners and administrators, faculty concerned with assessment at the department or program level, and faculty and staff charged with the responsibility of assessing the general education experience.

Despite promising to keep things simple, Barbara Walvoord is never simplistic in her presentation. She acknowledges the complexity of learning and of the assessment that must match its features. While endeavoring to keep assessment "simple, cost efficient, and useful," she encourages faculty to set ambitious goals for student learning, even if they may seem ambiguous in terms of their measurement potential. She urges that we not fall into the trap of discarding goals like preparing students to become ethical decision makers and good citizens just because these abilities seem difficult to measure. Even today we can employ questionnaires and interviews to ask current students and recent graduates if they perceive that they have experienced growth in these areas as a result of their college experiences, and in future years we can operationalize these concepts and develop more direct measures of associated behaviors.

When faculty are confronted with the necessity of creating an assessment initiative to satisfy a state or board of trustees' mandate or the requirements of an accreditor, they often respond—quite rightly—"Aren't we already assessing student learning? After all, we evaluate student work and give grades." One of the many features of this work that I admire is Barbara Walvoord's willingness to identify and respond to legitimate concerns about outcomes assessment. In this case, she not only acknowledges that faculty and student affairs staff on every campus are engaged in assessment but includes in every chapter the vital step of completing an audit of all the assessment activities already in place and asking how the use of the data from these activities to improve student learning could be enhanced. In her prior presentations and publications, Barbara has become well known for her advocacy of the use of rubrics to make meaning of grades in the outcomes assessment process. In this volume, we are treated to new examples of rubric construction and of the use of classroom assessment techniques in the quest for data that can help us improve instruction and ultimately learning.

In reviewing such a brief work, my greatest concern was related to the limited ability to provide context for the steps to be taken in inaugurating and sustaining an assessment initiative. Assessment approaches are unique, due primarily to the diverse organizational structures and background experiences, expertise, and personalities of instructors and student affairs staff that constitute the environments on different campuses. Barbara has addressed this concern by providing examples and options for proceeding in a variety of contexts, and in the appendices, specific illustrations designed for a variety of institutions.

Barbara Walvoord gives us detailed examples of reporting formats applicable at department and institution-wide levels. She urges that responses to assessment findings be based on the best current theories of student and organizational growth and development, then cites references that can be helpful in the search for such theories.

I could say more, but I am reminded of Barbara's emphasis on brevity. My overview, then, is designed simply to whet your appetite for the rich educational experience that lies in the pages ahead. Happy reading!

Trudy W. Banta

About the Author

BARBARA E. WALVOORD, PH.D., is Concurrent Professor Emerita at the University of Notre Dame. She has consulted and led workshops on assessment, effective teaching, and writing across the curriculum at more than 350 institutions of higher education. She coordinated Notre Dame's re-accreditation self-study. She founded and directed four college and university faculty development centers, each of which won national recognition. She taught English and interdisciplinary humanities courses for more than thirty years and was named Maryland English Teacher of the Year for Higher Education in 1987. Her publications include *Effective Grading: A Tool for Learning and Assessment in College,* 2nd ed. (with V. J. Anderson; Jossey-Bass, 2010); *Teaching and Learning in College Introductory Religion Courses* (Blackwell/ Jossey-Bass, 2008); *Academic Departments: How They Work, How They Change* (with others; ASHE ERIC Higher Education Reports, Jossey-Bass, 2000); *In the Long Run: A Study of Faculty in Three Writing-Across-the-Curriculum Programs* (with L. L. Hunt, H. F. Dowling, Jr., and J. D. McMahon; National Council of Teachers of English, 1997); and *Thinking and Writing in College: A Naturalistic Study of Students in Four Disciplines* (with L. P. McCarthy in collaboration with V. J. Anderson, J. R. Breihan, S. M. Robison, and A. K. Sherman; National Council of Teachers of English, 1990).

Assessment Clear and Simple

Chapter 1

For Everyone
The Basics of Assessment

YOU PROBABLY ARE reading this book because you are an administrator, department chair, assessment director, general education committee member, or faculty member involved in assessment. I wrote this book after serving in several of those administrative and faculty roles myself and serving as a consultant on assessment for more than 350 institutions, public and private, large and small, traditional and nontraditional. I have written this book for all those people and their institutions.

The Purpose of This Book

This book provides a short, clear, no-nonsense guide to assessment. The book examines how assessment can serve departmental and institutional goals—not merely external mandates—and how assessment can be conducted effectively and efficiently with ordinary peoples' available time, expertise, and resources. This book aims to make assessment simple, cost efficient, and useful for student learning, while meeting the assessment requirements of accreditation agencies, legislatures, review boards, and others.

Relation to Other Resources

I have emphasized brevity and practicality. Other types of resources for assessment include collections of case studies such as Banta, Jones, and Black (2009) and longer books such as Suskie (2009), a very thorough guide at more than 300 pages. My and Anderson's *Effective Grading* (2010) focuses on classroom assessment, including establishing goals, designing assignments, encouraging student motivation, designing the course, communicating with students about their work, and saving time in the grading process. It forms a kind of Venn diagram with this book, because its final section discusses how to use student classroom work, as well as other measures, for assessment in departments or general education programs.

The Organization of This Book

This book is organized in the following way:

- This chapter, which everyone should read. It defines assessment, answers common concerns, and lays the groundwork for each of the following chapters.
- Chapter Two, for institution-wide leaders and planners: assessment directors and committees, provosts, deans, and anyone who wants to see the "big picture" for the institution.
- Chapter Three, for department members and chairs.
- Chapter Four, for general education leaders and faculty.

Themes of the Book

The following themes recur throughout this book:

- Assessment is a natural, scholarly act that can bring important benefits.
- Assessment is composed of three steps: goals, information, action.
- The end of assessment is action.
- Assessment involves communicating across cultures, within and outside the institution.
- You need not only individual data collection, but systems for feeding data into decision making.
- Build on what you're already doing.
- Use students' classroom work, evaluated by faculty, as a valuable source of information about learning.
- Keep it simple!

What Is Assessment?

Assessment is the systematic collection of information about student learning, using the time, knowledge, expertise, and resources available, in order to inform decisions that affect student learning.

Assessment as a Natural, Scholarly Act

Assessment is a natural, inescapable, human, and scholarly act. When we spend time teaching students how to shape an argument or solve an equation, we naturally ask, "Well, did they learn it?" Our academic training urges us to look for evidence to support claims, so when the college catalogue claims that students learn to be critical thinkers, we ask, "Well, do they?"

We're Already Doing Assessment

Assessment is so natural we have been doing it all along. Whenever a department or program says, "Students' senior capstone projects showed that, as a group, they are not doing well on X. Maybe we could . . ."—that's assessment. It happens all the time in responsible departments and programs.

Assessment as a Reform Movement

Assessment is a powerful national reform movement. The movement draws from public dissatisfaction with the perceived shortcomings of college graduates. Proponents of assessment believe that higher education should examine what students have learned, not just what the institution or department did that supposedly resulted in learning. The movement has become a mandate, imposed by accreditors and by some boards and state legislatures. Issues of accountability and public disclosure have become conflated with assessment (Ewell, 2004). It's a complicated scene. To follow the national movement, consult Ewell (2008) and the pages of the monthly newsletter *Assessment Update,* especially the columns by Ewell (www.interscience.wiley.com).

Movements and mandates may present both opportunities and dangers. Faculty often voice fears that appropriate faculty control over what is taught and how it is tested will be curtailed; results of assessment will be used irresponsibly; standardized tests will drive instruction; the goals of higher education will be dumbed down to what is measurable only in a narrow sense; higher education will be held responsible for things it can't control, such as the students' previous education or their lack of motivation; or educators will be forced to create costly and time-consuming bureaucratic systems that comply with accreditors' demands for assessment but that do not really result in improved student learning. These are real dangers. But the answer is not to ignore assessment, resist it, or leave it to others. Instead, *we must improve our assessment systems so that they help us enhance student learning, draw upon the best aspects of academic culture, and are sustainable in terms of time and resources. Then we need to explain our assessment systems clearly and without arrogance to our various constituencies.* I believe that we and our students can profit from assessment while minimizing the dangers. The purpose of this book is to show how.

The Three Steps of Assessment

The good news is that accreditors ask us to follow three steps that are natural and scholarly:

1. *Goals.* What do we want students to be able to do when they complete our courses of study? (Goals may also be called "outcomes" or "objectives." Issues of language are discussed later in this chapter.)

2. *Information.* How well are students achieving these goals, and what factors influence their learning? (Information may be called "measures" or "evidence.")

3. *Action.* How can we use the information to improve student learning? (Using the information may be called "closing the loop.")

Sometimes an additional step is added between 2 and 3: identifying where in the curriculum the goals are addressed (sometimes called "curriculum mapping"; see example in Appendix A). This step is not assessment per se, because it focuses on what the institution or department does to bring about student learning, not on what the students learned. Nevertheless, curriculum mapping is useful to identify goals that are not being consistently addressed. The three steps of assessment are discussed in detail within this chapter and the other chapters in this book.

Classroom Assessment and Program Assessment

Classroom assessment takes place within the confines of a single class. The instructor examines student work, talks with students about what worked for them, and then makes changes to his or her pedagogy or classroom activities.

Program assessment involves the department, program, general education, or institution examining student learning within those larger arenas and then taking action. For example, a department may examine a sample of capstone research projects from its senior undergraduate majors, as well as results from a senior student survey, in order to determine where the department can improve students' learning within the program as a whole. A general education committee may examine student work from a sample of general education courses, not to evaluate each teacher's performance but to assess how well the general education program as a whole is meeting its goals.

The End of Assessment Is Action

The goal of assessment is information-based decision making. To put it another way, *the end of assessment is action.* Assessment helps the organization determine how well it is achieving its goals and suggests effective steps for improvement.

That means you should conduct assessment for yourselves and your students, not just for compliance with accreditors. You don't need to build a whole superstructure of assessment bureaucracy; it's much more important to incorporate good assessment into all the institution's core decision-making processes that are already in place: departmental decision making, committee deliberations, administrative policies, budgeting, and planning. You don't need to collect data you don't use; it's much more important to collect a small amount of useful data than to proliferate data that sit in a drawer or on a computer file. If you are collecting information you are not using, either start using it or stop collecting it. Instead of focusing on compliance, focus on the information you need for wise action. Remember that when you do assessment, whether in the department, the general education program, or at the institutional level, you are not trying to achieve the perfect research design; you are trying to gather enough data to provide a reasonable basis for action. You are looking for something to work on.

The Most Common Actions Resulting from Assessment

Three common actions that result from assessment in the department, in general education, and in the institution are these:

1. Changes to curriculum, requirements, programmatic structures, or other aspects of the students' course of study
2. Changes to the policies, funding, and planning that support learning
3. Faculty development

Sometimes the first action from an assessment is to gather additional information.

Pitfalls of Assessment

Common pitfalls of assessment include

- Mere compliance with external demands
- Gathering data no one will use
- Making the process too complicated

Section Summary

- Assessment is a natural, scholarly act, asking, "Are students learning what we want them to?" and "How can we better help them learn?"
- Assessment is also a national movement that poses both potential dangers and great promise for improving student learning.
- Assessment has three steps: goals, information, and action.

- The purpose of assessment is informed decision making.
- Assessment can go wrong when it focuses on compliance or on complex data gathering without using the information for decision making.

Concerns About Assessment

Aren't Grades Assessment?

Yes. But grades by themselves have limited use for program assessment. A department might know that the average grade on student senior research projects was 3.6, but that doesn't tell them much. It's not enough to say that we know students learned X if they got a grade of C or better in such-and-such a course. Instead, the department needs more specific, diagnostic information: students were strong in X and Y, but weak in Q and R. That detailed information tells the department what to work on. Such detailed information may emerge as faculty are grading student work, but then it must be aggregated and analyzed at the department or general education level, as each chapter in this book explains.

Sometimes grades can be used as a red flag. Especially, departments may want to monitor the grade distribution in introductory courses.

> Example: *Uncomfortable with the proportion of D and F grades and withdrawals from the introductory General Chemistry course at the University of Notre Dame, faculty members, led by Professor Dennis Jacobs, began a more extensive assessment. Faculty analyzed students' performance on the common chemistry exams and students' math Scholastic Aptitude Test (SAT) scores; they conducted interviews and focus groups with students; and they examined the research literature on how students most effectively learn in science. The grades were a red flag; the faculty used other data to expand their understanding of what was happening. Their findings and actions led to significant improvement in student learning (Jacobs, 2000, and Jacobs's Web site at www.nd.edu/~djacobs).*

How Can We Assess Complex Learning?

Assessment can and should be applied to the learning that the department, program, or institution most values, including the inclination to question assumptions, sensitivity to poverty and injustice, scientific literacy, the ability to work effectively with people of diverse backgrounds and cultures, or the development of ethical reasoning and action (for one list of liberal learning outcomes, see www.aacu.org/leap/vision.cfm).

We can't fully assess such ineffable qualities, but we can get indications. We are not caught between "objectivity" (in the sense that all judges of a student performance will agree on its quality) and "subjectivity" in the sense of individual whim. Between those two poles stands informed judgment of work in our fields. As professionals, we assess our colleagues' work all the time. Assessing students' work is part of that responsibility. In assessing student work, not all judges of a single piece of student work will agree on its quality, but that's how disciplines move forward. If raters disagree, assessors can use established methods: take the average score, ask another rater to break the tie, or have raters discuss the student work to see whether they can come to agreement.

To get indications about how well our students are achieving ineffable goals, we must rely on student work or student actions that may offer only a small window into the ineffable quality. For example, suppose you want students to develop "ethical reasoning and action," which is one of the essential liberal learning outcomes identified by the LEAP (Liberal Education and America's Promise) project of the Association of American Colleges and Universities (www.aacu.org/leap/vision.cfm). To assess whether your students are developing this quality, you might rely on two methods:

1. Ask them in surveys whether they believe your program helped them develop ethical reasoning and action.
2. Evaluate something they do.

Under these two headings, many options are available. For example, Gelmon, Holland, Driscoll, Spring, and Kerrigan (2001) compare and contrast a variety of methods for assessment of aspects such as "awareness of community" and "sensitivity to diversity" that may result from students' service learning.

> Example: *Columbus State Community College faculty asked students to write about a scenario; the writings were evaluated for ability to "value diversity" (Hunt, 2000).*

• • •

> Example: *The United States Military Academy assesses students' "moral awareness" through analysis of classroom work, student surveys, and employer feedback (Forest and Keith, 2004).*

If your accreditor requires that you construct "measureable objectives," you don't have to abandon your high goals; you just have to identify, within the larger goals, some more concrete goals or "objectives" that can be applied to the student work you will analyze. For example, some departments, addressing the overarching goal of students' ethical behavior, choose to measure whether students follow the ethical principles of the discipline as they conduct research and write papers. Others choose to measure whether students can identify and discuss ethical issues in case studies or scenarios. These measures do not address the entire concept of "ethical behavior," but they give indications about whether students are achieving aspects of your broader goal.

Can Assessment Be Applied to Online and Accelerated Learning?

Yes. Assessment gathers information about student learning, no matter what the pedagogy or mode of communication. If students are weak in a certain concept, the remedy may be somewhat different in an online course than in a face-to-face course, but the basic assessment process is the same.

Does Assessment Violate Academic Freedom?

The Association of American Colleges and Universities' Board of Directors Statement on Academic Freedom and Educational Responsibility (2006) directly addresses the issue of assessment and academic freedom:

> There is, however, an additional dimension of academic freedom that was not well developed in the original principles, and that has to do with the responsibilities of faculty members for educational programs. Faculty are responsible for establishing goals for student learning, for designing and implementing programs of general education and specialized study that intentionally cultivate the intended learning, and for assessing students' achievement. In these matters, faculty must work collaboratively with their colleagues in their departments, schools, and institutions as well as with relevant administrators. Academic freedom is necessary not just so faculty members can conduct their individual research and teach their own courses, but so they can enable students—through whole college programs of study—to acquire the learning they need to contribute to society.

Does Assessment Violate Student Privacy?

You do not need permission from your institutional review board (IRB) for normal assessment procedures described in this book. Federal policy exempts "(1) Research conducted in established or commonly accepted educational settings, involving normal educational practices, such as (i) research on regular and special education instructional strategies, or (ii) research on the effectiveness of or the comparison among instructional techniques, curricula, or classroom management methods. (2) Research involving the use of educational tests (cognitive, diagnostic, aptitude, achievement), survey procedures, interview procedures or observation of public behavior." *However*, you must be sure that individual students cannot be identified and that they would not be harmed by disclosure of their responses outside the research (U.S. Department of Health and Human Services, 2008).

If you are conducting assessment for a grant-funded project or for publication, or if you have any doubts, check with your IRB. You are free to use the student permission form in Appendix B of this book, which I developed for a published study that used students' classroom work, journals, surveys, interviews, and classroom observations to explore teaching and learning in undergraduate introductory religion courses (Walvoord, 2008). This form passed the human subjects review boards of sixty-two institutions, ranging from public research-intensive universities to small private liberal arts colleges. Another example—a consent statement used for a grant-funded program to study critical thinking at Washington State University—appears in Maki (2004, p. 197). For a discussion of special issues in medical schools, see Brainard (2004).

Will Assessment Be Used in Tenure and Promotion Decisions?

Assessment is an evaluation of student learning to determine what faculty as a whole can do to improve that learning. A wise institution keeps the focus on collective action, not on individual blame. Keep a barrier between personnel decisions, which require administrative action and which protect personal privacy, and, on the other hand, program assessment, which requires collegial action by the department or institution. If assessment reveals a problem that can only be addressed by getting rid of a faculty member or changing his or her individual teaching practices, move that problem to the personnel side, and choose another problem for departmental assessment action. My usual advice is not to use student course evaluations both for personnel decisions and for program assessment. Develop a different instrument for programs—one that asks students how the program as a whole has contributed to their learning, or how it could be improved. Later chapters contain more details about these methods.

That said, an individual faculty member may use information about student learning as part of evidence for tenure, reappointment, or promotion. Evidence of learning can balance low student evaluations, for example. But the opposite is also true. Evidence of inadequate student learning in one's class ought to galvanize the teacher and the department for appropriate action. That action must be collegial and supportive, just as it optimally is when a faculty member is not producing sufficient research. The truth is that assessment brings to teaching a level of accountability that was not always present before. The issues are complicated. The goal, however, is that assessment should be a collegial effort aimed at working together, as a team, to improve student learning.

Student Learning Is Affected by Factors Beyond Faculty Control

True, it is. But faculty, departmental, and institutional decisions do affect learning. A wise assessment program focuses on those factors you can control. For some audiences and purposes, you may also want to gather information about factors beyond your control, such as students' incoming skill levels or the number of hours they spend at their jobs, in order to establish students' beginning points or to present a fair picture of the context for student learning in your institution.

Section Summary

- Grades are only minimally useful for assessment; much more important are evaluations of the strengths and weaknesses of student work.
- Assessment can address complex learning.

- Concerns about assessment must be handled thoughtfully, but they need not be roadblocks to effective assessment.

Benefits of Assessment

Faculty sometimes ask, "Is there any research that shows that student learning improved as a result of assessment?" Yes and no. It would be impossible to design a research study that investigated whether, overall in the United States, student learning has improved because instructors and institutions are now being asked to do assessment in more explicit ways than before. There are too many variables; the meaning of "student learning" in that question is too broad; and assessment has always been occurring, even if not called by that name. Further, it's not the assessment itself that leads to improvement, but the action taken. The child's growth comes not from weighing her, but from feeding her.

What *can* be said, however, is that in countless individual instances, in departments and institutions of all types, assessment has been well used as a tool to help faculty and institutions make decisions that affect student learning, and that in some of those cases, the department, program, or institution has collected evidence that the new actions appear to have enhanced students' learning. In 1993, Banta surveyed assessment coordinators at 115 institutions to collect their stories of how assessment findings had been used for improvement. She bemoans the lack of controlled longitudinal studies to track improvement in learning (one could still bemoan that lack), but some of the individual cases, even at that early time, offer documentation of improvement after assessment-informed actions. More recent collections of case studies include Banta, Jones, and Black (2009); Bresciani (2007); the journal *Assessment Update* and the edited collections of *Assessment Update* articles published by Jossey-Bass; and case histories of institutions that have improved learning and cost-efficiency in basic courses under the National Center for Academic Transformation (www.theNCAT.org).

Finally, "Does assessment improve learning?" is the wrong question anyway. We have to make decisions about curriculum, policies, resources, and pedagogies. We can make those decisions *with* information about student learning or *without* it. People have always sought information to inform their actions. In higher education, assessment is the answer to the latest educational fad, because it asks that we gather information about how well students are learning and that we use that information to inform our actions rather than just go along with what's currently in vogue. Assessment gives us another basis for action besides what people think would work, what other people do, or what's in someone's self-interest or convenience.

The right question is, "Since of course we want viable information to inform our actions, what information do we need, and how can we effectively gather, interpret, and use it?" In times of severely limited resources, we need assessment more than ever. When money is tight, time is stretched to the limit, and we're at our wits' end, we should not be saying, "We don't have time or resources to do assessment." Instead, we should be saying, "Let's use well-conducted assessment to help us achieve our aims most efficiently in this difficult time."

Section Summary

- We naturally want good information about student learning to inform our actions.
- Assessment, when well conducted, can help us gather that information and use it effectively.

- When used effectively, assessment can lead to improvement in learning.

Communicating About Assessment

We not only must do assessment well, but we must communicate about our assessment to accreditors and other external audiences. Each chapter of this book discusses how to write assessment reports and self-studies; this section lays down the general principles that guide such communication.

Assessment Is Cross-Cultural Communication

Assessment is an exercise in cross-cultural communication among various segments of the academy and between the academy and those it serves. Bergquist and Pawlak's *Engaging the Six Cultures of the Academy* (2008) describes the cultures that coexist on most campuses and that influence how "assessment" is named, perceived, and used. I would place the assessment movement primarily within the "managerial" culture, which values the articulation of goals and objectives for students' learning, purposeful planning to achieve those goals, and the use of data to evaluate the achievement. Assessment also contains aspects of the "developmental" culture, which seeks to further the intellectual and personal development of both students and faculty and which relies on institutional research for information about this development. Many faculty, on the other hand, are part of the "collegial" culture, marked by high value on disciplinary research, high insistence on faculty autonomy, and ambiguity toward accountability for student learning. Each culture, however, has aspects that overlap the others, and individuals may function as members of multiple cultures. People in all cultures may care deeply about student learning, and each culture has ways of conducting assessment, though they may not use the word. Good communication about assessment can be built by looking for common ground, addressing various audiences with language that is accurate and familiar to them, and being honest.

Who Needs to Know *What*, for *What*?

It is easy to focus solely on accreditors as the audience for assessment, but assessment information may also be useful to potential students, donors, the general public, legislature, board, and others. The most important audiences may be your own students, faculty, and administrators. Audience and purpose should direct your choice of assessment methods: Questions such as "Should we use portfolios?" or "Should we use a standardized test?" can be answered by determining "Who needs to know what, for what?" Appendix C is intended to help you plan for your audiences.

Accreditors Are Not the Enemy

The regional accreditors are subject to federal oversight; from many directions, they feel pressure to be tough on assessment. Accreditors' staffs and funding are stretched thin. Critics have proposed that they be abolished and replaced with a single national accrediting agency staffed by educational measurement experts, instead of the current visiting teams comprised of faculty and administrators from other campuses. If we want to keep our peer review system, it's in our best interest to help our regional accreditors do their jobs. Treat them not as the enemy, but as colleagues and collaborators.

Use Self-Reflective Analysis

An accreditation study is not a public relations piece but a candid analysis. When I coordinated the writing of the self-study for my own institution, every section had a description of our actions in that particular area, followed by a section headed "strengths," a section headed "weaknesses," and a section headed "future plans." If you try to cover up weaknesses, or puff up your report, the accreditors are tempted to turn into "gotcha" police. Instead, you want to enlist these visitors as colleagues in candid conversation about the strengths and weaknesses of your current system and what can best be done to improve it.

Section Summary

- In communicating about assessment, consider the needs of your audience, recognizing that you may have to cross cultural lines.
- Ask "Who needs to know what, for what?"
- Adopt a self-reflective posture. Seek collegial conversation with those who are asking you for assessment.

General Guidelines for the Three Steps

This section presents some general guidelines that underlie the more specific advice that appears in later chapters for institutional leaders (Chapter Two), department chairs (Chapter Three), and general education (Chapter Four). I have arranged the guidelines under the three steps—goals, information, and action—but the purpose here is not to give a complete guide to the three steps themselves but to present those general principles that are common to all levels of assessment and that I do not want to repeat in each following chapter.

Guidelines for Establishing Goals

The first step of assessment is to establish learning goals. This section lays down some common principles; each successive chapter discusses how to establish goals in its particular domain.

Format: "Students Will Be Able to . . ."

Goals must be in the "students will be able to . . ." format. Here are some goal statements that are *not acceptable* for this purpose (though they may be perfectly fine statements for other purposes):

- The curriculum emphasizes X, Y, Z.
- The institution values X, Y, Z.
- The institution prepares its students for X, Y, Z.
- Students are exposed to X, Y, Z.
- Students participate in X, Y, Z.

Terms: Goals, Objectives, or Outcomes?

I use the term *goals* throughout, but in various settings, you will find other terms such as *objectives* or *outcomes* (student learning outcomes are sometimes referred to as "SLOs"). These terms are used inconsistently in the literature, so don't get hung up on the distinctions. Trying to get a whole faculty to understand and consistently employ a particular distinction among these terms may be futile. I suggest choosing one term, such as *goals*, with the understanding that the goals must be stated at various levels of generality. If your accreditor, board, or system is using any of these terms with a specific meaning, good communication practice would suggest that you use their terms when you write for them.

Levels of Generality

You will state the goals at various levels of generality. For example:

- *Institutional level.* Students will communicate effectively in writing to a variety of audiences.
- *Department/school/college level.* Students who complete the business major will communicate effectively to professional and lay audiences, using the common business formats.
- *Course level.* When they complete this finance course, students will be able to write such-and-such kinds of financial reports.

Subsequent chapters discuss goals for the institution as a whole (Chapter Two), for departments (Chapter Three), and for general education (Chapter Four).

Section Summary

- State goals as "students will be able to ..."
- The terms *goals, objectives*, and *outcomes* are used inconsistently in the field; keep it simple; meet the needs of your audiences.

- Goals must be stated at different levels of generality for different levels of assessment.

Guidelines for Gathering Information

The second step of assessment is to gather information about how well students are achieving the goals. Again, subsequent chapters show specifically how to accomplish this step in the institution, departments, and general education. Next are principles for two common types of direct measures: standardized tests and classroom work. Each has its own benefits and drawbacks.

Standardized Tests

Assessment per se does not require standardized tests; it asks for a sensible combination of measures that will yield useful, actionable information about student learning, including some direct measures. Standardized tests offer scores that can be compared to national samples, and they test students against national standards of performance. Seeing how your students perform against a national standard may provide bragging rights or it may be a shock. Both can be useful. However, if your students score low on the test, you have no way to improve their scores unless your faculty are willing to teach what the test is measuring. In addition, standardized tests may present other methodological problems. If the test does not count toward regular academic work, students may not do their best. Getting a meaningful sample of students to take the test can be difficult. Tests are expensive. Chapter Two discusses in more detail the institutional decision about administering a national standardized test and about joining collaborative agreements, such as the Voluntary System of Accountability, to make scores public.

Classroom Work: Samples and Portfolios

Classroom work, like standardized tests, has advantages and limitations. One advantage is that classroom work is already being examined by faculty as part of the grading process, so evaluating it for assessment purposes can be time efficient and relatively inexpensive. Classroom work carries a grade, so students may be more highly motivated than if they took a standardized test that did not count in their grades. Classroom work reflects what students actually are taught at your institution, rather than what standardized test constructors think should be taught. Faculty may be more invested in their own analysis of students' work than they are in the results of some standardized test. And classroom work can be evaluated in many ways over time, to yield many kinds of insights.

On the other hand, classroom work does not yield scores that can be compared across institutions. And it takes careful work to aggregate classroom work or portfolios so that the results can be used for action in the department or program, general education, or the institution as a whole. The next sections of this chapter discuss aspects of using classroom work that are common to all situations. Succeeding chapters discuss in more detail how classroom work may be used for institutional, departmental, and general-education assessment.

The final chapters of my and Anderson's *Effective Grading* (2010) also discuss how to aggregate and use classroom work for assessment in grant-funded projects, departments, and general education. Also useful is Banta's (2003) collection of *Assessment Update* articles about portfolio uses, cases, scoring, and impact, and Zubizarreta's (2009) useful book on portfolios, including their uses in classrooms.

Gathering Student Classroom Work. Depending on your assessment questions, audiences, and purposes, you should give careful thought to the amount and type of student work you need to collect. Here are some common selections:

- Penultimate work from a course toward the end of the students' course of study. For example, a capstone research paper, concert, theater performance, or internship. Answers questions such as, "What are students' strengths and weaknesses at the end of our program?" An excellent starting point for any assessment program. From this work, select a weakness to work on, and, if necessary, gather further information from earlier student work.
- Pre-post: Sample of student work at the beginning of their course of study and at the end. Answers questions such as, "What is the 'value added' for students in our program of study?"
- Portfolios of student work (a *portfolio* is multiple pieces of one student's work completed across time). Answers questions such as, "How do our students develop?" or "How well can students exhibit particular skills in a variety of settings?"

You can gather student work (either samples or portfolios) in two ways:

1. Ask a sample of faculty to submit copies of their students' work and/ or to analyze their students' work.

Example: *The Office of Institutional Research identifies each year a random sample of general education courses that are focusing on, say, critical thinking. The chosen course instructors submit their student papers for an assignment that asked for critical thinking. These papers are evaluated by a group of faculty readers who produce a report that is disseminated among general education faculty and used at the institutional level for action to improve the general education program. A process similar to this one was used at Johnson County Community College in Kansas (Seybert and O'Hara, 1997).*

· · ·

Example: *In a department, instructors of 400-level courses that ask for research papers are asked to submit rubric scores or analyses of the strengths and weaknesses of their own students' work, measured against one or more departmental learning goals. These reports are aggregated to inform departmental decision making.*

2. Ask a sample of students to submit their work.

Example: *A random sample of students are contacted and asked (or paid) to submit copies of their work. Interviews or other information may also be gathered to provide a deeper set of data.*

· · ·

Example: *Software may be used to collect student work. As students submit their work online, they give permission for their work to be used as part of a sample for assessment. Assessment projects can then select a sample from the online work.*

· · ·

Example: *Students in a capstone course compile portfolios as part of their coursework. The portfolios are used for department or general education assessment.*

Establishing Criteria for Evaluating Student Work. When you evaluate student work, you need a set of criteria or a set of questions. You can use a rubric or an alternative method.

The rubric is a format for expressing criteria and standards. The advantage of a rubric is that it disaggregates various qualities of the students' work. Thus it is diagnostic; it helps you see what to work on. Instead of "Students' average grade on the capstone project was B+," a rubric helps you say, "On the capstone project, students' strengths were P and Q, and their weaknesses were X and Y."

Rubrics can be minimal or full. A minimal rubric simply lists the traits on which the evaluation will be based, and it indicates a scale, but without describing the student's performance at the various levels of the scale (Exhibit 1.1).

Minimal rubrics may help a group of faculty identify what they value, but you won't get very high percentages of interrater reliability (instances where readers give the same paper the same score). You also won't get much detail about what is going wrong if, for example, students score low on "organization."

A full rubric addresses these problems. It describes each level of performance. Exhibit 1.2 is one section of a rubric developed for assessing essays in which students were to take a stand on a debatable issue about a work of literature (full rubric is included as Example 1 in Appendix D).

A rubric may be used as the basis for a grade by weighting the various traits (for example, thesis counts 25 percent, support counts 40 percent, and so on), or the rubric may simply be shared with students as a guide to their work, not necessarily correlating numerically with a grade. *Effective Grading* (Walvoord and Anderson, 2010) discusses in detail how to share

---

EXHIBIT 1.1
Minimal Rubrics

Option 1. Naming the Traits

Thesis	5	4	3	2	1
Organization	5	4	3	2	1
Etc.					

Option 2. Describing the Top Performance

Thesis is clear, debatable, complex, and creative.	5	4	3	2	1

EXHIBIT 1.2

Selection from a Full Rubric for Essay of Literary Analysis

5	4	3	2	1
Thesis: The thesis of the paper is clear, complex, and challenging. It does not merely state the obvious or exactly repeat others' viewpoints, but creatively and thoughtfully opens up our thinking about the work.	The thesis is both clear and reasonably complex.	The thesis is clear, though it may be unimaginative, largely a recapitulation of readings and class discussion, and/or fairly obvious.	Thesis is discernible, but the reader has to work to understand it, or the thesis seems to change as the essay proceeds.	Thesis is irrelevant to the assignment and/or not discernible.

grading criteria with students and how to relate rubrics to grades. A basic principle is that, if you're using a rubric, it should be shared with students before they begin the assignment or test.

Rubrics may be constructed either by individuals or by groups such as a department or a general education committee. Steps for constructing rubrics and answers to frequently asked questions about rubrics can be found in my and Anderson's *Effective Grading* (2010), which places rubrics in the larger context of course planning and pedagogy. Within a more narrow context, Stevens and Levi (2005) offer a guide to constructing and using rubrics. For examples of how rubrics have been used for program assessment, see Case Study 2 in Chapter Three of this volume, the case studies in Chapter Twelve of *Effective Grading,* and many of the case studies in Banta, Jones, and Black (2009), in Bresciani (2007), and in the various collections of *Assessment Update* articles edited by Banta and published by Jossey-Bass (Banta 2004, 2007a, 2007b; Banta and Associates, 2003).

While I was teaching hundreds of faculty to construct rubrics, I have found that some faculty take to rubric construction immediately, and ask, "Why didn't I start using rubrics years ago?" Other faculty, who may be equally smart and equally good at teaching, find it hard to bend their thinking into a rubric format. If you're not comfortable with rubrics, then use a list of criteria and analyze the students' work for strengths and weaknesses. As you read each paper, make a list of the strengths and weaknesses it exhibits in meeting the criteria. (If you're just beginning to shape criteria, let the criteria statements grow and change as you do this.) At the end, aggregate the lists of strengths and weaknesses to find those most common to the papers as a whole.

> Example: *A group of philosophy faculty read a selection of senior student research papers, jotting down notes about the papers' strengths and weaknesses as they read, and then identifying the overall strengths and weaknesses of the group of research papers as a whole. Faculty took their written notes to a meeting of all the readers, where, in conversation, they identified the strengths they wanted to celebrate and one student weakness they wanted to work on. No rubrics were used, but the process yielded action based on careful faculty analysis of student work.*

• • •

> Example: *At one institution, a sample of fifty students from various disciplines were paid to assemble portfolios containing selected pieces of their work across four years (their first paper from their first semester college seminar, the last paper in that seminar, what they judged to be the best paper of their second semester, the first paper they wrote in a course in their major, and their best paper from a senior course in their major). These were combined in the portfolios together with annual interviews conducted by a researcher, annual surveys completed by the student, and transcripts of the student's coursework and grades. A group of ten faculty were offered stipends during the summer, each to read ten complete portfolios. (Thus, each portfolio was read by two faculty members.) The faculty readers were asked to address a set of questions that the group had determined ahead of time, but they were also asked simply to note what struck them or surprised them about the portfolios. What themes and patterns emerged? What were points of contrast and comparison? Then the group of ten faculty met for broad-ranging discussion about what they had found—a discussion that was eventually narrowed to identify several areas for further investigation by more focused techniques. This strategy employs the broad "What's going on here?" question used by qualitative researchers as they initially survey a broad range of data.*

Aggregating and Analyzing Student Work. Classroom work (samples or portfolios) can be aggregated for use by the department, general education, or the institution in either of two ways (Figure 1.1).

In Option 1, the instructor (piggy-backing on the grading process) prepares a report of students' strengths and weaknesses or rubric scores on

FIGURE 1.1

Evaluating Student Classroom Work: Two Options

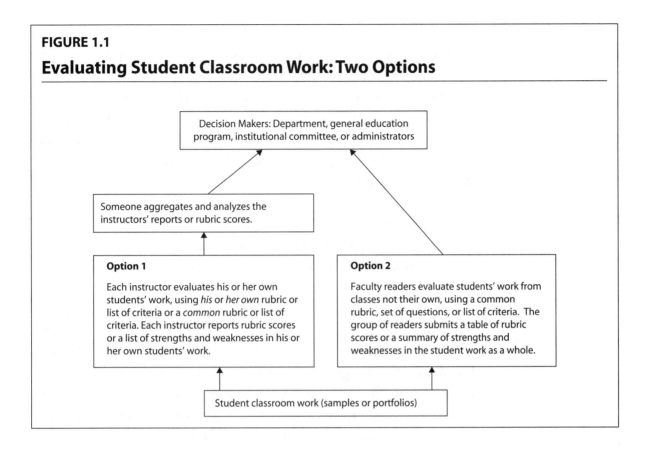

one assignment or a portfolio of assignments for the class as a whole or for some predetermined sample of class members. These individual instructor reports are then aggregated. For example, one might examine fifty faculty members' reports to discover which student weaknesses are most often mentioned. This is the least time-consuming method of gathering classroom data because the papers are read only once—by the instructor. Everything else is based on the instructor's report or rubric scores.

In Option 2, the instructor may play no role or may serve only as the collector of student work, not the analyzer. The pieces of student work or portfolios are read by a separate group of readers (usually faculty but sometimes graduate students), who prepare a single report for the department or general education. This method introduces external eyes, but the faculty readers may not understand what they are reading. Moreover, Option 2 is more time consuming, because each piece of student work is read twice—once by the instructor for a grade, and again by the faculty readers for assessment.

If you are evaluating pieces of work or portfolios that are *similar* to one another in type and discipline, you may use either of the two options. However, if the student work is *different* (for example, you are trying to evaluate critical thinking or writing skills from student work in disparate courses such as history and physics, or work of disparate types such as the case study and the research report), it may be very difficult and time consuming to follow Option 2, the common rubric used for all the student work. Before you embark on constructing a common rubric for varied types of student work, ask yourself why you need a single set of rubric scores. Read the case study of Tompkins Cortland Community College (Cameron, 2009) for a description of the five years of arduous work involved in constructing and using a single rubric for disparate work, and the ongoing difficulties with interrater reliability, as well as the benefits of this process for faculty.

You don't have to use a single common rubric to evaluate disparate types of student work. An alternative is to construct (or adapt from elsewhere) a general rubric or a set of criteria or learning goals to be used only as a *guideline* and let disciplinary groups construct their own discipline-specific or assignment-specific rubrics and/or lists of criteria based on the general guidelines. Then you take the individual rubric scores or lists of strengths and weaknesses, and aggregate them, looking for common themes or for difficulties that are most often mentioned. Such an aggregation can serve as the basis for action. If many of the individual rubric scores or lists of strengths and weaknesses show difficulty with using appropriate online sources, work on that. If they show difficulty in considering alternative solutions/explanations/arguments, work on that. For general rubrics that you might be able to adopt or adapt, follow the work of the Association of American Colleges and Universities (www.aacu.org) and the Teagle Foundation (www.teagle.org).

Section Summary

- Standardized tests are not required for assessment. Use them if they yield information you can act on.
- To state criteria and standards for student work, you can use rubrics or alternatives such as lists of criteria.
- To evaluate student work, you can have individual instructors evaluate their own students' work and then aggregate those evaluations, or you can have a group of readers evaluate student work that is not their own.
- Using a single rubric for disparate work is difficult; an alternative is to use a general rubric or set of criteria as a guide, and let individual departments or instructors create their own assignment-specific versions.

Guidelines for Action

The third step of assessment is to act on the information—sometimes called "closing the loop." Each succeeding chapter discusses how to close the loop in various situations; this section presents general principles.

Identify Factors Affecting Learning

Knowing the strengths and weaknesses of student work does not necessarily tell you what to *do* to improve student learning. For that, you need information and hypotheses about what is affecting student learning. You will probably use two ways to collect this information and formulate hypotheses:

1. Rely on the research that is already available.
2. Do some research yourself.

The research that is already available tells you what factors are likely to be affecting your own students' learning, and what actions might help. For analysis of the institutional characteristics linked to student success, consult Kuh (2008), Kuh and others (2005a, 2005b, 2007), and Pascarella and Terenzini (2005). A study of church-related colleges is Braskamp, Trautvetter, and Ward (2006). For the teaching methods that research has found most successful for learning, consult Chickering and Gamson (1987), which is widely available on many Web sites. For a given situation, more specific research may be helpful. Then let the published research guide and complement your own investigation.

> Example: *Teaching the general chemistry course we mentioned earlier, which was trying to help a greater proportion of its students be successful in the course without lowering the standards, faculty consulted the research literature to identify possible causes of students' failure and to find teaching methods that had worked in other settings. The faculty also analyzed students' tests, interviewed students, and examined their SAT scores. The literature, as well as the department's own research, suggested that some students had not learned the problem-solving strategies that were necessary for college-level chemistry, and that the large lecture format was not very effective for these students. The research suggested that integrating small-group problem-solving and frequent graded homework problems would enhance students' problem-solving skills. The department implemented those strategies, and a greater percentage of students did better on the same final exam. (For the case history on which my short incident here is based, see Jacobs, 2000, and www.nd.edu/~djacobs).*

Are the Actions Working?

If you were to "close the loop" in a scientific way, you would not only use assessment information to inform your action, but you would then come back and examine whether your action was achieving the improvement of student learning you had hoped. The chemistry department was able to do just that, by comparing students' scores on the common final exam, to see whether students in the experimental section did better than a matched group of students taught by the old pedagogies.

This type of reexamination to see whether a strategy worked can be effective in departments or in individual general education programs such as the required math or composition class. The scale is often small enough to track the impact of changes on student learning. However, suppose a general education program noted, from standardized test scores, student surveys, and/or faculty review of portfolios, that students' writing skills were not what the faculty had hoped. The institution consults the research literature, interviews students, examines how writing is being taught across its curriculum, and takes significant steps to address the writing issue. Could the institution, five years later, expect that these changes would result in an improvement in students' writing scores on a standardized test or on faculty-scored portfolios? The institution would certainly want to continue to track the test and portfolio scores, but there might be so many variables at work, so many other changes taking place over time, and such a large, complex population of students, that no significant difference in overall scores would appear. That doesn't necessarily mean the changes were worthless; it may simply mean that there are too many variables, and the nature of "writing" is simply too different in different disciplines and contexts. In that situation, one might investigate smaller settings: for example, take ten individual courses in various disciplines in which faculty adopted new pedagogies to enhance student writing. Investigate whether student writing improved in those courses, using samples of student writing in each course.

Further examples and details about "closing the loop" are presented in the chapters that follow.

Section Summary

- To inform your action, you need information and hypotheses about the factors that affect learning. Gather these from the published literature and your own investigation.
- If your context is too broad or complex to track whether specific changes are producing improve-

ment in learning, you can take a sample of local situations, such as individual classes or programs, where improvement in learning can more easily be tracked.

Okay, So What Should We Do?

People often ask me for a specific list of "what we should do" for assessment. The lists below are not necessarily exhaustive, but they provide a framework for how each segment of the institution could do assessment in ways that are helpful to decision making, consonant with natural and scholarly processes, and acceptable to accreditors and other external audiences.

Classroom instructors could

- Articulate what we want students to be able to do when they complete our courses
- Gather information about student learning from our own classroom assignments/exams, and from surveys, focus groups, or conversations with our own students about their learning experience, and use that information to improve student learning in our own classes
- Be willing to bring that information to the department or general education program to be aggregated with other classroom information and used for decision making in areas where problems needs to be addressed at levels beyond the individual classroom
- Keep records of our assessment work and report that work as needed

Departments or programs could

- Articulate what students should be able to do when they complete each of our certificate or degree programs and our general education and service offerings
- Gather information from a sample of students' classroom work, from student feedback, and from other sources as relevant, and use that information for decisions and actions that affect student learning
- Be willing to bring our information to other decision-making committees, offices, or administrators, so it can be aggregated with other information and used for decision making.
- Keep records of our assessment work and report that work as needed

General education programs could

- Articulate what students should be able to do when they complete the general education curriculum
- Develop subgoals for individual general education programs such as the composition program, the math program, learning communities, or community-based learning
- Gather information from a sample of students' classroom work, from student feedback, and from other relevant sources, and use that

information to make decisions about general education curriculum and policies, and/or to offer faculty development

- Be willing to bring that information to other decision-making sites
- Keep records of our assessment work and report that work as needed

Faculty committees, governance bodies, and administrators could

- Support assessment efforts with resources, policies, and encouragement
- Ensure that the institution has a consistent, integrated assessment system that uses information about student learning for improvement at every level—department, general education, and institution as a whole
- Keep records of assessment work and report that work as needed

---

Chapter Summary

- The end of assessment is action.
- Pitfalls of assessment include merely complying with external demands, gathering data no one will use, and making the process too complicated.
- Grades are only minimally useful; instead, you need diagnostic information about students' strengths and weaknesses.
- *Goals, objectives, outcomes*—don't sweat the terminology. Just state "students will be able to . . ." at various levels of generality.
- Standardized tests may be necessary for accountability, but if you have a choice, examine your options very carefully. Consider using student classroom work.
- Students' classroom work is a valuable source of information about learning, if you evaluate it by rubrics or lists of criteria.

- It is very difficult to use a single common rubric for varied types of student work. Consider using the generic rubric as a guide, and letting individual programs or instructors generate their own assignment-specific rubrics.
- To act on information about learning, you need research and hypotheses about the factors that may affect learning.
- Do your best to track the results of changes you make. In large, complex contexts, you can choose a sample of classrooms or programs to show results of changes.
- What to do: Follow the three steps: goals, information, action. Put in place a sensible, sustainable assessment system that helps you improve student learning, then explain your system to accreditors.
- Keep it simple!

Chapter 2

For Institution-Wide Leaders and Planners

THIS CHAPTER IS aimed especially at those who are responsible for the "big picture" of assessment at the institution: provosts, deans, assessment directors, committee members, faculty governance leaders, and others who have responsibility for the system of assessment at the college or university. The chapter addresses both those who have well-developed assessment systems and those who are just getting started. It assumes that you have read Chapter One.

The chapter first discusses how to establish a vision, audience, purpose, and learning goals. Then it shows how to analyze your current assessment system. Succeeding sections of the chapter discuss each of five common improvements that institutions make on the basis of their analyses. These include improving (1) the "digestion" of data, (2) the quality of departmental assessment, (3) the collaboration between academic and student affairs, (4) the use of standardized tests and surveys, and (5) the use of student classroom work, whether in samples or in portfolios. In the two final sections, the chapter discusses how to report your data to accreditors and how to budget for assessment.

Establish Vision, Audience, Purpose, Goals

Establish a Campuswide Vision for Assessment

The aim of assessment is not compliance with accreditors—its goal is *informed action* that enhances student learning. An important role of assessment leaders is to help shape and reinforce that vision of assessment.

- Every public statement about assessment, whether written or oral, should reinforce the vision of assessment as a necessary and natural act that helps the campus achieve its most important goals.

- Put visible resources behind assessment. If finances are very tight, a small amount of new money has a high symbolic value. The visibility of the support is as important as the amount.

Example: A dean at a small community college that was experiencing severe financial cuts established an assessment budget with funds from the dean's own (small and diminishing) discretionary budget. Departments and programs could submit proposals for how they would use this money to enhance assessment processes or to act on assessment results.

• Tie assessment to resources and processes that count—program review, budget requests, general education review or reform. Assessing student learning should be the foundation of all these processes. More about this later in the chapter, as we discuss the campuswide assessment system.

The rest of this chapter discusses how to implement a campuswide assessment system that instantiates the vision. First, identify audience, purposes, and campuswide learning goals. Then analyze your current system for assessing student achievement of those goals. Make improvements to that system. Describe the system to accreditors and others.

Identify Your Audiences and Purposes

It is easy to assume that accreditors are the only audience for assessment. As Chapter One advises, let the question, "Who needs to know what, for what?," guide your assessment planning. Assessment is not about collecting data; it's about who needs the information for what purposes. The end of assessment is action. Appendix C offers a template for planning.

Establish Learning Goals for the Institution as a Whole

You cannot assess students' learning unless you have articulated what you want that learning to be. Review the basic principles for establishing goals in Chapter One. This next section shows how to construct learning goals for the institution as a whole. Later chapters discuss how to formulate learning goals in the department and in general education.

Setting Different Goals for Different Schools or Campuses

When the institution includes very different schools, such as a medical school and a law school, or a two-year institution embedded within a university, or when the institution operates on multiple campuses with different missions, you may have a very broad mission statement or broad set of learning goals for the whole institution, but I would concentrate on constructing a meaningful set of learning goals for each distinct college or campus, because these goals can be specific enough to guide assessment and action, and the college or school is likely to be more invested in assessing goals it shapes for itself.

Relating Goals to Mission

The goals must be related to the institution's mission statement. Two common problems may arise:

1. The mission statement or existing goal statements are not couched in the "students will be able to . . ." format.
2. The mission statement contains highly abstract goals.

Here is a mission statement that illustrates both problems: "The college strives to promote tolerance, lifelong learning, and devotion to free inquiry and free expression to ensure that its graduates are individuals of character, more competent to contribute to society, and more civil in habits of thoughts, speech, and action."

You need a set of learning goals that makes these statements more specific and more manageable. You might try to change the mission statement, but do that only if you think the campus will benefit from that process. The "students will be able to . . ." goals do not need to replace current goal or mission statements. They can simply be placed on the institution's Web site along with these other documents. For example, a committee could generate learning goals under the broad heading "character," "civility," and "societal contribution." These might include the usual competencies that appear in most institution-wide learning goals: students will develop skills in critical thinking, quantitative reasoning, ethical decision making, global awareness (or cultural competence), oral and written communication, information literacy, technological competency, and the like. Some accreditors dictate broad areas you must include.

These goals might simply be used as the committee's version of the mission. Or you might want to give the goals a somewhat more formal status by asking various campus bodies to endorse the goals. Keep it simple; get it done. Then you can move to gathering information about how well students are achieving the goals.

> Example: *At a community college with a very abstract mission statement, the assessment committee fashioned a set of "students will be able to . . ." goals that they used as their interpretation of the mission. No further formal action was taken; the assessment committee's goals were placed on the assessment Web site along with the mission and were used as the basis for assessment.*

• • •

> Example: *At a large research university with a very abstract mission statement, the assessment committee drafted a set of "students will be*

able to . . ." goals, discussed them with the appropriate committee of the academic council (the governance body with faculty, administrative, and student members), revised the goals according to the council's suggestions, and then asked the council of each college (Arts and Sciences, Law, Engineering, and so on) to vote to accept the goals, which they did. These goals were then placed on the university Web site and used as the basis for assessment. The goals were shared with the board of trustees, but the goals were treated as an explanation of the mission statement and did not require board approval.

Finding Resources for Shaping Institutional Learning Goals

If you have yet to fashion goals in the "students will be able to . . . " format, here are some resources that will help:

- *Gather your own institutional documents.* Begin by gathering the mission statement and whatever other relevant documents the institution has already constructed. Don't neglect statements that may have emerged from previous self-studies, fund-raising campaigns, reports to a board or legislature, or other events that may provide greater sharpness or detail than the mission.

- *Consider accreditors' guidelines.* You might adopt your accreditor's guidelines or some version of them. For example, the New England Association of Schools and Colleges (NEASC) specifies, "Graduates successfully completing an undergraduate program demonstrate competence in written and oral communication in English; the ability for scientific and quantitative reasoning, for critical analysis and logical thinking; and the capability for continuing learning, including the skills of information literacy. They also demonstrate knowledge and understanding of scientific, historical, and social phenomena, and a knowledge and appreciation of the aesthetic and ethical dimensions of humankind" (New England Association of Schools and Colleges, 2005, Standard 4.18).

Not every regional accreditor is this specific, but the NEASC guidelines reflect elements present in most goal statements. If you are accredited by NEASC, you can construct your own versions of the goals, provided each of the mentioned general areas is represented.

- *Consider AAC&U resources.* The Association of American Colleges and Universities' LEAP (Liberal Education and America's Promise) project has articulated a set of "essential learning outcomes" of a "liberal education." (http://www.aacu.org/leap/vision.cfm).

- *Search online.* Many institutions post their goal statements online, accessible to the public. These statements often reflect widely held values in higher education; it's okay to adapt or adopt someone else's statement.

Relating Institutional Goals and General Education Goals

Regional accreditors will want to see written goals at the level of the institution, general education, and department or program. The general education goals may simply repeat some of the institution-wide goals, or they may be more specific versions of the relevant institution-wide goals. Chapter Four discusses these options in more detail.

The Goals Must *Live!*

Once you have a set of institution-wide learning goals, put them on the institution's Web site. Use them as the basis for lower-level goals by departments, student services units, and general education. Emphasize that these goals must *live*!

> Example: *I consulted with a campus whose senate had just passed a new set of institutional learning goals in preparation for the institution's upcoming reaccreditation review. The committee that drafted the goals had spent a great deal of time, had attended a workshop sponsored by AAC&U, had consulted the emerging literature on liberal learning goals, and had become very invested in this goal statement. The senate had trusted the committee to take care of this accreditation requirement and had passed the goals with little discussion. The goals sounded fine. They had some stuff in there about global perspectives and lifelong learning—what's not to like?*
>
> *A few weeks later, I arrived on campus to lead a workshop to help departmental teams work on their departmental assessment systems. As a first step, I asked the departments to formulate, review, or revise their learning goals. They were to use their disciplinary values, but also they were to consider how their department goals addressed the new university-wide goals. Some department members were astonished that the institution-wide goals would actually have to be addressed within departments. Global perspective, lifelong learning—we haven't explicitly addressed these goals, they said. So together we began the long process of making those institutional learning goals real within the academic programs and talking about how the academic side and the student affairs side would need to collaborate more closely to address these complex goals.*

Section Summary

- Clarify your audiences and purposes for assessment.
- Translate vague mission statements into "students will be able to . . ." goals as expeditiously as pos-

sible so you can move on to assessing student achievement of the goals.
- Above all, the goals must *live!*

Analyze Your Overall Assessment System

Once you have campuswide learning goals in place, you need a campuswide system to assess how well your students are achieving these goals and to inform decisions at every level, from the classroom and department on up to the provost, president, and board. You probably have already reported your assessment to accreditors, and/or you have taken some steps to implement assessment. But a frequent mistake educators make is to pile up pieces of assessment without taking stock of the whole picture. Campuses frequently ask me, "Should we administer standardized tests?" "Should we use e-portfolios?" "Should we purchase assessment software?" You should answer such questions *only* within the context of your overall system of assessment. This section of the chapter shows how to analyze your system.

Diagramming Your Assessment System

Because assessment is about making information-based decisions, a useful tool for mapping an institutional assessment system is a diagram that tracks how data about student learning flow into decisions throughout the institution. Creating such a diagram helps you to analyze and improve your assessment system. A diagram can also be included in your reaccreditation report to address the criticism so often made by accreditors—that the institution has pockets of good assessment but no overall system.

Figure 2.1 shows a diagram created by an institution to reflect its current system of assessment—a system with some problems, as analysis later in this chapter will show. Figure 2.2 shows an ideal system.

These diagrams are read from the bottom up. The figures' basic structure highlights three aspects:

1. *Data.* What are the various kinds of data you have about student learning? Represented in the bottom boxes of the figure.
2. *Digestion.* How are these data "digested"—that is, aggregated, analyzed, and disseminated? Represented in the middle of the figure.
3. *Decisions.* How are these data used for decisions, policies, planning, and budgeting? Represented at the upper levels of the figure.

FIGURE 2.1

A Problematic Assessment System

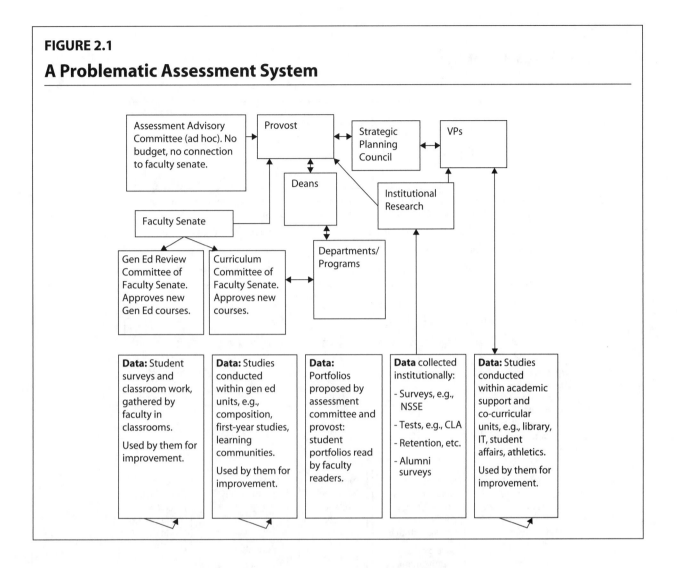

Analyzing Your Assessment System

Note that the difference between the problematic system and the ideal system lies not primarily in the data collected but in the way the data are used—the number of arrows that show data flowing to decision-making sites. Further, the ideal system has a large central box I call the "stomach," which performs the "digestion" of data so it can be well used for decisions. Most institutions I visit need work on the "stomach."

You can ask whether you have enough data and the right kinds of data. Next, ask about the arrows. Where are useful data dead-ended without arrows leading to decision-making sites? Where are decisions being made without data that might be helpful? Also, pay attention to how data are digested: who aggregates, analyzes, and prepares the data for use by decision makers? One of the key differences between the problematic system of Figure 2.1 and the ideal system of Figure 2.2 is that the ideal system has a robust digestive

FIGURE 2.2

An Ideal Assessment System

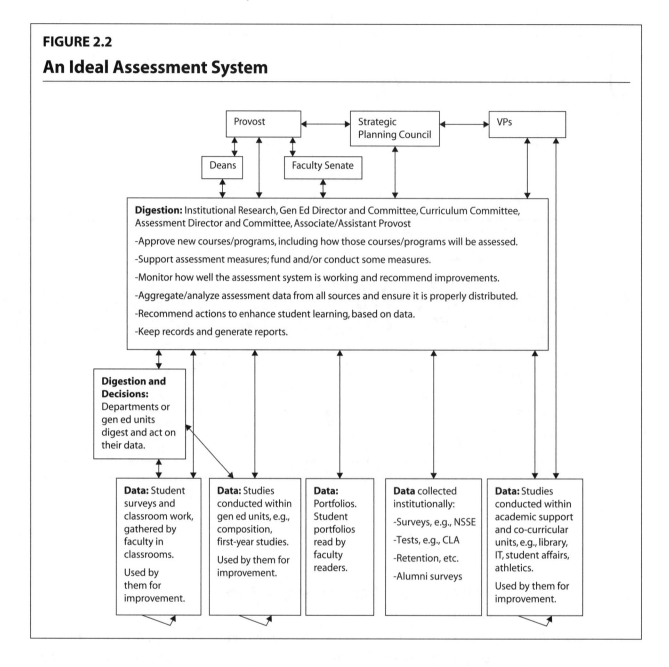

system. A related question: Is the assessment committee appropriately connected to key institutional processes and resources?

The institution represented in Figure 2.1 concluded

- We have plenty of data, both direct and indirect.
- Our classroom data are dead-ended; no one in the department or institution systematically uses what faculty members know about student learning based on faculty review of student work.
- We may spend plenty of time and money doing portfolios, but if they are dead-ended we will reap few benefits.
- The assessment committee lacks connection and power. Its function is unclear.

- Information about learning from student affairs and academic support units is separated from information about learning from the academic side. Who has a full picture of the learning of the whole student?
- Several "digestive" functions are not being fully accomplished: aggregating and interpreting relevant data, integrating various sources of data with one another, and ensuring that data summaries and recommendations are forwarded to the appropriate decision-making sites.

Many institutions will have problems similar to these. The following section discusses five types of improvements that institutions commonly make after analyzing their assessment systems. The institution represented in Figure 2.1 needed work on the first of these improvements—the digestion of data—as well as several other aspects.

Section Summary
• You need an overall system for your assessment.　• A diagram can help you evaluate your assessment system, improve it, and explain it to accreditors.

Make Improvements to the Assessment System

Improving the "Digestion" of Data

The first improvement that institutions often make after analyzing their assessment systems is to improve what I call the "digestion" or the "stomach" of the assessment system—the way in which data about student learning are aggregated, analyzed, and prepared for use by various decision makers. The institution whose problematic system is diagrammed in Figure 2.1 had been focusing on whether to add more data such as portfolios or a standardized test, but after analyzing their diagram, they decided to focus on improving the digestion of the data they already had.

As Figure 2.2 shows, there are six functions that must be well performed if the assessment data, shown in the bottom row of boxes, is to make its way into the decision-making sites of the institution. Those six functions are these:

1. *Approving* new courses and programs, and regularly reviewing general education courses, including the requirement that those courses are regularly being assessed
2. *Supporting* and *coaching* assessment efforts at the course, department, program, and general education levels

3. *Monitoring* the effectiveness of the overall assessment system and offering recommendations to improve it

4. *Aggregating*, *interpreting*, and *disseminating* assessment information to centers of decision making where they can be best used

5. *Recommending* ways to improve student learning, based on data analysis, and sending those recommendations to centers of decision making where they can best be used

6. *Keeping records* and *writing reports* about assessment to various audiences, internal and external

These functions must be performed by some combination of the following bodies:

- Assessment director
- Assessment committee
- General education director
- General education committee
- Curriculum committee
- Academic policies committee
- College and school deans and directors
- Provost's office
- Institutional research office
- Perhaps the Teaching and Learning Center (though it is important to keep the center a safe place where faculty can go to get help with their teaching, and where they can be candid about their teaching problems in full assurance of confidentiality. Some institutions keep the center entirely separate from program-level or institution-level assessment but ask it to work with individual faculty on classroom grading, teaching, and related topics)
- Special task force
- Event: Special meeting, conference, retreat, or summit

  Example: *One university instituted an annual half-day assessment retreat including representatives of provost's office, student affairs VP, assessment director, gen ed director, and deans, to examine assessment data and generate ideas for their own areas and for the institution as a whole.*

For many institutions, the most powerful improvement they could make in their assessment systems is not to add more data but to improve the functions of the "stomach." Exhibit 2.1 is a planning grid that might be useful in planning how the tasks of the stomach are performed. Don't just put an X into a cell; instead, insert a brief description of what the unit, committee, or office does. For example, in the row for the assessment committee,

EXHIBIT 2.1

Digestive Tasks for the "Stomach" of the Assessment System

Approving Courses/ Programs, Including Their Assessment	Supporting/ Coaching / Departments and Programs in Assessment	Monitoring Effectiveness of Assessment Systems	Aggregating/ Analyzing/Dis- seminating Assessment Data	Recommend- ing Action Based on Data	Keeping Records, Writing Reports
Assessment director					
Assessment committee					
Gen ed director					
Gen ed committee					
Curriculum committee					
Policies committee					
Deans					
Provost's office					
Institutional research					
Teaching center					
Special task force					
Event: Meeting, conference, retreat, or summit					

you might write nothing under "Approving," but under "Supporting" you might put, "sponsors workshops for department chairs; administers small grants to departments for assessment." Under "Monitoring," perhaps you would write that the assessment committee "annually overviews the assessment system and makes recommendations to the provost for more effective assessment." Under "Keeping Records and Writing Reports," perhaps the assessment committee "contributes data about assessment to the writer(s) of accreditation self-studies."

Do We Need an Assessment Committee?

Educators within institutions often ask me, "Do we need an assessment committee?" You should answer that question in the context of your analysis of the diagram, especially its "stomach." Here are several scenarios.

- A number of years ago, a research university had a provost who offered, at best, mixed messages about assessment and was himself skeptical about its usefulness. When the institution's regional accreditor asked it for a special report on assessment, the provost assigned this task to an assistant provost who did not hold a tenured position on the faculty. She dutifully went to several national meetings to inform herself, then visited every department with her message about how to do assessment. She was received with resentment in some quarters and with open hostility in others. Little progress was made, and the institution's report on assessment was again frowned upon by its regional accreditor. Then the provost appointed a faculty member as coordinator for assessment. The coordinator tapped several well-respected faculty colleagues to form an assessment committee. This committee was crucial to the success of the effort: they became the respected faculty colleagues who knew about assessment; they worked with their own colleagues to soften attitudes and get assessment processes started; and they urged the provost to give more consistent support to assessment.

- Fast-forward seven years. Same institution. Now they have a new provost who really gets it about assessment, and an associate provost who had served on the original assessment committee and also fully gets it. Both these administrators are respected by the faculty. Working through regular policy bodies, these administrators implement assessment strategies. Many of the recommendations of the original committee are now embedded into the institution's ways of operating. The original members have mostly gone off the assessment committee, and current members are not sure what their function is. The fire has gone out of the assessment committee, and its meetings are poorly attended. The associate provost who is in charge of assessment, the coordinator, and the committee itself decide that an assessment committee of the old type is no longer needed. Instead, two things happen: (1) both the curriculum committee and the academic policies committee appoint one of their members to represent the concerns of assessment in all deliberations; and (2) the associate provost and the coordinator form an ongoing series of ad hoc faculty groups or faculty-student groups who can work knowledgeably on particular assessment issues such as assessment in the first-year seminars.

- Fast-forward four years. Same institution. Now they're two years from a full review for reaccreditation. The institution is also embarking on a new round of strategic planning. As part of both these review efforts, the provost appoints an ad hoc committee to review the assessment system. The committee is charged with constructing a diagram such as that in Figure 2.2, making recommendations to the provost and the academic policies committee about how to improve the assessment system, and then helping to write the report to the accreditors.

- Different institution. Midsized private liberal arts college. The assessment committee began as a subcommittee of the curriculum committee. It got some good people, advocated effectively for assessment, and became a separate, standing committee. At that point, I was engaged as a consultant, and the committee asked me to help it clarify its role. We looked at the entire "stomach" of the institution. After considerable debate, the institution constructed a version of the "stomach" in which the assessment committee would have *all* the functions of the "stomach," including examining assessment data and making recommendations. This is a tough role for a faculty committee because of the expertise and time commitment it requires. However, the committee had the full support of the faculty, which had a long tradition of strong faculty governance, and of the administration, which provided released time for a faculty assessment coordinator, made secretarial support available, and ensured that a staff person with research experience would have time to work with the committee. Now the assessment committee is a very strong body, fulfilling all the functions listed for the stomach.

Improving Departmental Assessment

A second type of improvement that institutions often make after they diagram their overall assessment system is to improve the quality and usefulness of departmental assessment. Chapter Three of this book guides department chairs and faculty as they conduct assessment. This section suggests how institutional leaders can support that process:

- Embed assessment into central processes of the department's and institution's life
- Keep departments' workload down
- Offer support to departments

Embed Assessment into Central Processes

"I spent hours and hours on the assessment report," said one department chair, "and the assessment committee read it, patted me on the head for a good job, and that's all that ever happened." At least the assessment committee had read her report; many chairs tell me they believe no one reads their assessment reports. It's easy to focus on the reports as ends in themselves and fail to recognize that *assessment needs to flow into planning and budgeting.* Here are some ways to ensure that departmental assessment has meaningful consequences.

Program Review. If the institution has a meaningful program review process, it should include information about student learning as a basis for review and planning. Here is a logical sequence the review might follow:

1. Mission, vision, aspirations
2. Goals (what the program intends to accomplish) in areas such as research, community service, and student learning. Do not confuse goals with means. "Establish a new language lab" is a means to reach the goals of student learning, so only the *learning* goals should be listed here: When students complete their course of study, we want them to be able to . . .
3. Current resources for meeting the goals: demographic information, including numbers of types of students, faculty, staff, physical facilities, reputation, services and programs, and so on.
4. How well are we meeting the goals?
   a. Department's methods for gathering information about achievement of the goals, including methods of assessing student learning (see Chapter Three)
   b. Findings, including strengths and weaknesses in each goal area, including student learning
5. Plans for improvement, including enhancing student learning. Here's where to put "Establish a new language lab." The plan or request for the lab is presented as a way to meet learning goals, and the plan must be justified by evidence about how this step will help the department meet its goals for student learning.
6. Resources needed

Bresciani (2006) provides thorough guidelines and many examples of "outcomes-based program review" for academic and co-curricular departments drawn from a study of forty-three good-practice institutions.

Dangers of relying too heavily on program review for assessment of student learning are, first, that the program review might not occur frequently enough to enforce ongoing assessment, and, second, if the review concentrates on other issues such as the department's research standing, the assessment of student learning might get lost. You can deliberately structure the review to address these problems.

Example: *At one national research-intensive institution, program review committees were asked to designate one external reviewer chosen specifically for his or her expertise in student learning, who would be responsible during the review for attention to those issues. A portion of the six-month and three-year follow-up meetings between the department and the provost was dedicated to tracking the department's progress in enhancing student learning.*

Annual Reports. When departments report annually to the dean or provost, the report guidelines should include questions about how the assessment data are contributing to ongoing planning and action by the department.

Budgeting. As departments ask for faculty lines, staff, new facilities, equipment, or other resources, the relevant administrators can require data about student learning and a rationale for how the new resources will enhance student learning.

Separate Assessment Reports. In the best of all worlds, assessment would be so thoroughly embedded within the institution's core processes that the accreditors would need to examine only the program reviews, annual reports, and budget documents to see that assessment was at the center of institutional life. However, at present, most institutions compile separate reports about how their departments are doing assessment.

Many institutions establish a Web page to which departments contribute a two-page report for each program, degree, or certificate. Chapter Three gives details about these reports.

- Departments can use the Web page to share ideas about assessment.
- The writer of the accreditation self-study can draw from these reports to make statements such as "Eighty-nine percent of our departments have at least one direct assessment for each of their degrees," and "The most common types of indirect assessments our departments employ are . . . ," and "Every department has at least one example of how they have used assessment information to make improvements."
- The accreditors can be provided with the password to the Web page and can browse the page to get a sense of how departments as a whole are conducting assessment, or they can focus on a few departments in more detail.
- The page can be used as a basis for other audiences, such as the board or the state system.

You can offer a template or format as a guide for departmental reports. When I constructed such a Web site for my own university, most departments followed the common template, but a few departments preferred to use their own format, so their reports were simply posted on the web page as they were. It's not worth spending energy or fighting battles to get every last report in the same format.

There are software systems on the market that facilitate assessment, but the low-tech way for constructing this Web page of departmental reports requires only that you ask departments to send in the reports as Word documents. Then the provost's Web person or someone else with similar responsibilities can post the Word documents on the Web page. The page does not need to be fancy; it just needs to present the documents in readable form. An alternative is to set up a "class" in a course management system such as Blackboard and ask departments to post their assessment reports within that system.

Strategic Planning. As the institution begins a strategic planning process, each department can submit a one-page statement:

- What evidence about student learning they are using
- Strengths and weaknesses of student learning they have identified
- Actions they are taking or plan to take to enhance learning
- Issues about learning they believe the strategic plan should address

The provost or assessment office aggregates these departmental reports and generates a report about common issues, problems, and recommendations. This report is used by the strategic planners as one of their sources of information about what the institution needs. The reports allow the institution to capture the rich discussions that occur at the department level, based on classroom work and student input, and now aggregated and used for institution-wide planning and decisions. For a thoughtful analysis of the importance of using student learning information for strategic planning, and the reasons why more institutions don't do it, see Choban, Choban, and Choban (2008).

Gen Ed Review or Reform. As the institution begins gen ed review or reform, ask each department and general education unit (such as the writing program or learning communities) to identify two problematic aspects of students' work in that department's general education courses, measured against the institution's general education goals. The gen ed committee can aggregate these departmental or unit reports to identify the most commonly mentioned problems as a basis for planning how to improve student learning in general education. For example, writing, oral communication, or quantitative reasoning might appear as the most common problem that departments observe in their general education courses. Gaston and Gaff's *Revising General Education—and Avoiding the Potholes* (2009) is a practical guide.

Keep Departments' Workload Down

In every way possible, institutional leaders should acknowledge the extra work that assessment requires and keep that workload as small as possible. Keep the Web-based assessment reports down to two pages. Allow the department to use the same report as a section of its program review or budget request. Allow departments that are accredited within their disciplines to use those accreditation reports for the institution's regional accreditation. Above all, offer generous support to departments. Part of attending to workload issues is to provide as much help to departments as you can. Here are some suggestions.

Set Deadlines. My and my colleagues' study of how departments work suggests the power of deadlines to focus a department's efforts (Walvoord and others, 2000). Set regular deadlines for initial or updated assessment reports from departments. Don't let them wait because they're not ready. A department does not need to have a perfect system in order to have an assessment report. It simply reports in two pages what it is currently doing and how it plans to improve its system.

Offer Help in Completing the Report. You can help departments using a combination of three methods:

1. *Workshop.* Hold a three-hour workshop for teams composed of the department chairs and key faculty members. They should bring their current documents and their laptops. The workshop walks them through the three steps of assessment—goals, information, and action. By the end of the workshop, each department can have a written outline of an assessment report or a revision of a previous report for at least one of their programs—the two-year certificate, the undergraduate major, or a graduate degree. Then set a deadline, a month or two later, for them to submit the final report. You can videotape this workshop so those who miss it can watch it later.

2. *Interviews.* Have the assessment director or similar person interview each department chair, taking notes about the department's assessment. Write up the information as a two-page report, check it with the chair for corrections, and put it on the Web page. This is the most time consuming for administrators and the least time consuming for department chairs. I have done these interviews for thirty-five departments, spending about an hour with each chair. This technique is especially useful for departments that are hostile to assessment or that are doing assessment in ways

that are ineffective, overly complex, or grudgingly compliant, because you can address the department's issues directly.

3. *Resources.* Provide online or print resources and ask departments to compose and revise their own reports. If you provide this book to each department, suggest that they read Chapter One for an overall view of assessment and Chapter Three for departmental assessment. Offer online help in the form of a self-guided tour through the writing of the report, sample reports, and a help number to call.

Offer Rewards and Resources. The ultimate goal is that assessment is so embedded into the systems that affect the department's money, faculty lines, facilities, policies, or the provost's good graces that assessment carries its own rewards. Many institutions, however, operate with departmental budgets that are largely set by historical precedent, or with budgets that allow very few new resources. In those cases, there are ways outside the regular budgetary and planning system that an institution may establish rewards and incentives for assessment. Strategies might include

- Grants offered by the provost, dean, or assessment committee for departments that will produce model assessment systems and then coach other departments.
- An ongoing institutional or departmental budget item for assessment initiatives. So for example, at one institution, the English department assessed its required writing course and wanted to substantially revise it, so they asked for money to hold a day-long retreat off campus to get this work done. A department might want to offer summer stipends to two of its faculty to analyze senior student work. Another might want to administer a national standardized test and compare students' scores on that test with students' grades and their work in regular classes. Another might want to pay adjuncts a stipend for their participation in assessment activities. Another might want to order pizzas for a series of brown bag lunches to discuss how faculty could help students with an area of learning that had shown up as a weakness in the department's examination of student work.
- Responsiveness to needs discovered through assessment. The Allied Health Department at Anne Arundel Community College in Maryland examined its students' learning in a key required course, decided that they needed to provide better teaching materials for adjuncts teaching the course, and got support from their dean for these changes (see this case study in Walvoord and Anderson, 2010, Chapter Twelve).

Improving Collaboration Between Academic and Student Affairs

A third common improvement that institutions make after analyzing their assessment systems is to enhance collaboration between academic and student affairs. A significant body of research points to the importance of integrating a student's whole college experience and suggests ways to strengthen a culture of shared responsibility for student success (Kuh and Hinkle, 2002; Kuh, Kinzie, Shuh, Whitt, and Associates, 2005a; Kuh, Kinzie, Buckley, Bridges, and Hayek, 2007). Specifically in terms of assessment, it pays to ask how information about student learning from all sites, whether on the academic side or the student affairs side, is shared and used for decisions.

> Example: *One institution created a council on academic and student affairs that included vice presidents from both sides, as well as faculty and student representation, and that met regularly to share information, generate ideas, and try to ensure that the institution was providing for its students a coherent and integrated experience focused on the institution's learning goals and values.*

· · ·

> Example: *Another institution began to invite student affairs and academic support staff to the new faculty orientation, not just for each to give a five-minute presentation on their services, but for more extended small-group discussions of the institution's learning goals, some important data about the institution's students, and ideas about how faculty and student support services could work together toward common goals for students' learning and development.*

· · ·

> Example: *Academic and student affairs can collaborate in various programs, such as first-year student interest groups that help students integrate and make meaning from their college experiences (Schroeder, Minor, and Tarkow, 1999). It is important that faculty and student affairs staff involved in such collaborative efforts are well-equipped with assessment information about their institution's students—for example, the demographics, learning styles, modes of engagement, and so on. Further, the collaborative groups can themselves gather information about their impact on student learning, and their information can be shared with others.*

Improving Use of Standardized Tests and Surveys

A fourth improvement that institutions sometimes make after analyzing their assessment system is to add, drop, or improve their use of institution-wide standardized tests and national student surveys. Such tests and surveys are becoming more popular as sources of data about student learning. Consortial systems such as the Voluntary System of Accountability (VSA), sponsored by associations of public institutions, provide a common, online format in which public institutions volunteer to publish certain information including each institution's scores on a national student survey and its scores on one of three standardized tests (www.voluntarysystem.org). In addition, many institutions are making public their scores on the National Survey of Student Engagement or its companion for community colleges (www.nsse.iup.edu). Associations of private institutions, too, are moving toward greater public disclosure. I work with many institutions that believe they must administer standardized tests and surveys because others are doing so, because they belong to a state system that has decided to join the VSA, or for other reasons. Other institutions do not feel such pressures, but they wonder whether a standardized test or national survey would give them valuable information. Here are guidelines for considering and using such instruments.

Distinguish Between Accountability and Assessment

A key principle is not to confuse accountability with assessment. In a thoughtful essay, Ewell (2004) discusses the conditions under which public demands for "accountability," by which institutions demonstrate to external publics that they responsibly produce the expected results, might be congruent with "assessment," defined as "research . . . centered on learning outcomes . . . for the purpose of improving teaching and learning" (p. 105). Ewell's essay offers ways to clarify your own issues.

Understand Validity Issues

There is no perfect instrument to measure student learning. You'll want to know the methodological strengths and weaknesses of your chosen methods so you can use the information appropriately. Developers of standardized tests and surveys have validity information on their Web sites. For a knowledgeable critique of standardized tests, based on long experience using them institutionally, see Banta (2006, 2007c); Banta and Pike (2007); and Pike (2006). Pike (2008) discusses validity issues with the measures chosen for the Voluntary System of Accountability. Shermis (2008) evaluates the Collegiate Learning Assessment (CLA). Erwin (2004) explores various aspects of using tests for accountability.

Understand the Underlying Values

Currently popular national standardized tests and surveys, as well as rankings and benchmarks of various kinds, all have arisen from particular social and political contexts. "There simply are no value-neutral statistics in our business," says Ewell (2005, p. 194). Ewell's essay explores the values that inform the National Survey of Student Engagement (NSSE) and a number of other instruments and benchmarking systems; he suggests several aspects to look for in judging educational metrics. In another thoughtful essay, Shulman (2007) explores the "story" that various tests and surveys, including the NSSE and the CLA, are designed to tell. He offers seven "pillars" that should support good assessment. You can use both these essays to elucidate the values and stories that will inform your own choice, use, and dissemination of tests and surveys.

Understand "Value Added"

The term *value added* commonly refers to the concept that one can measure student performance at the beginning of a course of study, and at the end, calculate the difference between the two, and then ascribe the difference (the "value added") to the educational experience. The concept is intuitively appealing—hence its long history of recurrence in public debate and public policy about the quality of higher education. However, measurement experts have concluded that value-added assessment may have uses at local levels, but it is not a workable concept at the broader institutional level (Banta and Pike, 2007). There simply are too many variables at work, too many disparities in the concept of "learning," and too many methodological problems.

The alternative, I suggest, is the concept that guides this book: examine student performance at key points, particularly at the end of their course of study. Identify something you wish students were doing better. Explore the factors that influence that learning. Do whatever your research suggests will improve the learning. Look again, but don't necessarily expect that your actions will result in changes that show up in institution-wide measures.

Never Use Standardized Tests and Surveys as the Only Measure

Never let a standardized test and a survey be your institution's only way of looking at student work. Use student classroom work, evaluated by faculty, as another direct measure. Ideally, standardized tests and surveys will be one of several sources of data about student learning, each augmenting, correcting, and amplifying the others, to lead to appropriate action. Even those who construct and support standardized tests recognize their limits. Shavelson (2007) makes a case for using and indeed expanding the Collegiate Learning Assessment, but he also notes that "any large-scale assessment system can, at best, signal where a problem may exist, but it will not pinpoint the problem and generate solutions. For this, a campus needs to place any external assessment in the context of its own rich array of assessments and link it to institutional structures and processes" (p. 33).

Get Faculty Involved

Whether you are considering adoption of a standardized test or already have one in place, ask a dozen of your most respected faculty to take the test as if they were students. Ask them whether the test measures aspects of learning they believe are appropriate for your students and whether they believe their own classes help students do well on the test. Ask them to participate in the decision about whether, or how, to use the test in tandem with other kinds of information.

Consider Cost

All these standardized tests and surveys cost money. Part of the consideration is whether you already have enough information to decide what to work on. If so, perhaps you could make better use of the money. Perhaps you only need to administer a survey at intervals, or perhaps you can use a series of student focus groups to tell you what you need to know. Don't forget that most standard surveys offer the option of adding a few of your own questions at the end. Instead of administering another survey, can you add some questions to the one you already have?

Use the Test and Survey Data

The choice with the biggest impact is not which survey or test to administer. It's the choice about how you *use* the information. The National Survey of Student Engagement offers extensive guidance for using the results of their various student surveys to improve student engagement and learning (www.nsse.iub.edu). Their publication, *Using NSSE to Assess and Improve Undergraduate Education: Lessons from the Field 2009*, offers case studies that can be models for an institution's use of any tests or surveys. To augment these case studies, the following examples reinforce the importance of structuring the ownership, dissemination, and use of the data.

> Example: *The assessment coordinator was interviewing departments to find out what kinds of assessment they were conducting and to ask them what help they needed from the assessment or provost's office. The coordinator discovered that many chairs either did not know what*

institution-wide data were available or found those data too general to be easily applicable to their departments. As a result, the institution took two steps: (1) funding the Office of Institutional Research to expand the samples for the senior survey, to disaggregate the data by department, and to prepare reports that were more usable by individual departments; (2) devoting portions of chair orientation sessions to show chairs how to use the data; and (3) incorporating relevant questions about the data into the guidelines departments followed as they were preparing for program review.

• • •

Example: *A consultant arrived on campus to help with assessment. As part of her preparation, she had been shown data from the Collegiate Learning Assessment (a standardized test) and the National Survey of Student Engagement (a student survey). These instruments had been administered at the institution for several years. In talking with faculty and department chairs, the consultant found that only a few people knew what these instruments were or what the data suggested about the institution's strengths and weaknesses. The data were being collected at considerable cost but not fully used. As a result, the institution took a number of the steps such as those outlined in the NSSE case studies and in the Santa Fe Community College case that follows.*

• • •

Example: *At Santa Fe Community College, results from the Community College Assessment of Student Learning are examined by a work group composed of faculty from all four instructional divisions, staff from counseling and advising, and program directors from academic support units. The work group identifies patterns and concerns and reports widely to departments and offices across the campus. Thus the college immediately establishes ownership of the data by a wide spectrum of faculty and staff. Some findings have spurred quick action; other findings have been more difficult. Where the data are puzzling, the work group members, rather than make their own assumptions, show the data "as a teaser for faculty discussion and encourage the faculty to offer their own explanations" (Reynolds, 2007, p. 5). The case study offers considerable detail about the various hypotheses faculty proposed to explain one piece of puzzling data, and how these hypotheses were tested.*

Improving the Use of Student Classroom Work

A fifth improvement institutions often make after analyzing their system diagrams is to make better use of student classroom work to provide information about student learning. Chapter One discussed in general how to use student classroom work for assessment, whether you gather individual pieces of work or portfolios of student work completed over time. This section concentrates on the institutional leaders' and planners' role.

Should We Do Portfolios?

Portfolios, or e-portfolios, are widely discussed these days. The ideal scenario is seductive: students submit work throughout their college careers; at the end, the students will each have a wonderful collection of work that documents their progress in learning. The development of the portfolio can be tied to the advising system and to coursework, to provide an ongoing journey of learning aimed at clear learning goals. Individual instructors or groups of faculty readers can easily access student work online, assign rubric scores, and enter the scores directly into the computer, which can slice the data in many ways. That's the vision, but achieving anything resembling this ideal scenario will take very careful planning. Here's an example of a portfolio system that did not work:

> Example: *One institution had a couple of people in influential places who became champions for an institution-wide portfolio assessment system. One of the champions was the director of first-year seminars. Another was the director of computer support for faculty. They convinced the provost to purchase a software product to collect and track the portfolio items, and the computer center offered training sessions for faculty to learn how to use the software. The vision was that students would contribute to the portfolio from many of their courses, and that the developing portfolios could be used in a number of ways. Planners hoped that the availability of portfolios would make the advising system more effective and would provide a basis for assessment.*
>
> *The vision was only partly realized, however. Because the first-year seminar director was a champion for the project, most first-year seminar faculty helped students create appropriate assignments and enter them into the portfolio. A few departments began to use the portfolio system to assess the work of their majors. A few other departments had had portfolio systems already in place, on their own platforms, and those*

departments continued to use their own separate systems—a develop-
ment the planners had not foreseen because they had not known
about these quiet, department-based portfolio systems. Most faculty
ignored the portfolio system. After the students completed the
first-year seminar, they rarely kept up the portfolio. The institution had
not addressed the advising system as a whole, so other weaknesses in that
system prevented the portfolios from being well used for advising.

When I arrived on the scene, the computer folks were still spending
hours of their time maintaining the software and helping faculty use
it, but now the software producers wanted the institution to pay more
money for an updated version of the software, and in a budget crunch,
the provost was not sure he wanted to part with that money.

Keys to portfolio success can be identified if we contrast the previous
example with the portfolio system at institutions that have used portfolios with a measure of success. These include the Rose-Hulman Institute
of Technology (www.rose-hulman.edu), LaGuardia Community College
(www.lagcc.cuny.edu), and Truman State University (http://assessment.
truman.edu), presented in the following example. Other guides or
case studies about portfolios include Banta and Associates (2003) and
Cambridge (2001).

Example: *Truman State University's system has its own strengths and*
weaknesses, but a few key features contrast with the system described in
the previous example. Truman State requires every student to submit a
portfolio—not merely to complete first-year seminar, as in the previous
example, but to graduate. A significant, meaningful student requirement
is an important key to success. At Truman State, most students compile
their portfolios in a capstone seminar, where the instructor guides them.
Students draw from past work, without needing to involve the instruc-
tors of those past courses. Students also write a reflection on their work.
To analyze the more than 1,000 portfolios, more than fifty faculty readers
gather together during three summer weeks. The rubric scores these read-
ers assign are aggregated, analyzed, widely disseminated on campus, and
used for action. The assessment system has been ongoing for more than a
decade (http://assessment.truman.edu).

Though several key traits distinguish Truman State from the trou-
bled portfolio system described earlier, Truman State's Web page reports
acknowledge several ongoing problems: students sometimes cannot find
their best earlier works or never got them back from the instructor; students say they were never challenged in the designated intellectual area the

portfolio requirements stipulate, so they have nothing to submit (students may feel frustrated by this, but the information helps the university identify what students have and have not done); some students compile the portfolios and reflections hastily. Interrater reliability is an ongoing issue, as faculty raters differ from one another, even after training and norming. To address these problems, Truman State is moving toward allowing students to submit items to their portfolios from their first semester, creating a Web-based storage drive so students are less likely to lose papers as they move through the process, and collecting early and late responses on three prompts of special campuswide interest: critical thinking and writing, interdisciplinary thinking, and public speaking (Alberts, 2009).

The lesson is that if you are going to do institution-wide portfolios, you must

- Make completion of the portfolio very important to students.
- Provide a setting in which students can be guided to compile and reflect on their work.
- Allow for completion of the portfolios despite varying levels of support from faculty.
- Embed the portfolios system within other systems such as advising.
- Engage a number of key faculty with whom you can work intensively to support the portfolios.
- Carefully train and norm the readers.
- Ensure that the readers' reports are disseminated widely, owned by the campus at large, and used for action at many levels.
- Live with some methodological problems such as students' lack of investment, faculty lack of cooperation, and difficulties with interrater reliability.
- Keep working and changing to address problems and improve the system.

Alternatives to Institution-Wide Portfolios

Before you leap into institution-wide portfolios, consider whether your needs might be served by a smaller, more limited analysis of student work.

In the next example, the institution was able to build upon a small, local project undertaken within a single program.

Example: *The writing program director, as part of his regular duties for assessment of the writing program, decided to follow twenty-five students from their required first-year composition course throughout their four years, to find out how their writing instruction served them in following courses. From his own budget, he hired an adjunct instructor to work with him on the study. They paid the twenty-five students to submit all their writing, to be interviewed twice a year, and to allow inclusion of the students' demographic information, grades, and transcripts. The director and the adjunct developed a coding scheme and paid graduate students to code portions of the data. The findings were used to make significant changes in the writing program, which already had an extensive faculty development program for its adjuncts and a semester-long pedagogy course for all its graduate student instructors.*

So far, this is program assessment, not broader general education assessment. How do they make these results effective at the level of the institution? The director generated a report for the institution. It suggested that, in subsequent courses, students were not being fully challenged for the argumentative skills that the first-year course was teaching them. The report was brought to the Arts and Sciences College Council and to the provost. They reviewed the requirements for "writing-intensive" courses, publicized them more effectively to the faculty who were teaching the courses, and asked the writing program and the teaching/learning center to offer a series of workshops on designing writing assignments, helping students build on their first-year writing course, and giving feedback to students about their writing.

In this example, the small sample of students provided a manageable subset. The project was begun and funded within a single program, though the composition director might easily have appealed to the college dean or the provost for some extra funding to pay the adjunct or the graduate student coders. No extra software was needed. The drawback to this study is that very few faculty were involved until the report came out. The results were used fully in the composition program for real change but not as fully within the university as a whole. In retrospect, one wonders what would have happened if a large group of faculty had been offered stipends to spend just one day, in which they each read and analyzed a few portfolios, viewed the results of the director's coding, held a discussion in which they generated action items, and appointed some of them to work with the writing program director to bring the information to the campus at large.

My point in these examples is that portfolios are complicated. It is very important to fully consider:

- Do we need portfolios from every student or only from a few?
- What is the motivation for students?

- What is the motivation for faculty?
- Can we separate coding done by a few trained people from portfolio reading done by many?
- How will the results be owned and acted upon?
- What resources can we realistically provide over time?

Section Summary

The section has discussed several types of improvements the institution might want to make after it analyzes its assessment system. These changes include improving the following:

- "Digestion" of data
- Quality of departmental assessment

- Collaboration between academic and student affairs
- Use of standardized tests and surveys
- Use of student classroom work, whether in samples or in portfolios

---

Documenting Assessment for Accreditors and Others

While you are creating your assessment system, you will need to document it for your accreditors. For reporting to a regional accrediting agency, here's what I suggest you construct and document, not just prior to an accreditation visit, but all along the way:

- *Goals.* A set of learning goals, in the format "students will be able to . . ." at the level of
  - The institution
  - Each distinct degree/course of study (for example, the music performance major, the music history major, the masters in music education, and the Ph.D. in music history)
  - The general education program and each segment of it (for example, the writing program, learning communities, service learning, and so on)
  - Each individual course (accreditors vary in the emphasis they place on having learning goals in the syllabus for every course)
- *Overall system.* A diagram such as that in Figure 2.1. You should diagram the system that you have, with all its weaknesses. Then explain the diagram fully in your self-study or report, point out the weaknesses or limitations, and discuss how you will address them.
- *Departmental assessment.* A Web page that contains a two- to three-page description of the assessment process for each distinct degree or course of study, including graduate and undergraduate degrees,

certificates, and tracks within the major (for example, music history and music performance). The Web page can be password protected for your faculty and administrators; when accreditors need to review your assessment, you give them the password. The Web page need not be fancy. It can be part of the assessment Web page or part of the provost's Web page. You'll also need copies of your guidelines for departmental annual reports and program reviews, showing that assessment of learning is incorporated into these processes. You'll need a sample of departmental annual reports and departmental self-studies for program review, showing how departments are asked for assessment within these processes. Be honest; include some reports and self-studies that do it all wonderfully, some in the middle, and some that totally miss the mark. Point out the strengths and weaknesses. Discuss how you plan to help departments do a better job.

- *General education assessment.* A description of how the institution assesses its general education program, together with supporting documents.

- *Assessment in student life and academic support units.* A description of how assessment of student learning is used for decisions in all the units that affect learning, for example, library, instructional technology, financial aid, residence life, career counseling, and so on. This book does not go into detail about assessment in these areas, but it urges collaboration among all the offices that contribute in any way to student learning.

- *Strengths and weaknesses.* A candid evaluation of the strengths and weaknesses of your assessment data and your assessment system. This evaluation should occur throughout all your descriptions. Tell *everyone* on your campus: An accreditation report is not a public relations piece. It should not read like a recruitment brochure. Its tone should be evaluative, reflective, self-critical. You want to point out your own strengths and your own areas of weakness or challenge. The purpose of your tone is to create, in the minds of the accreditors, a picture of your institution as responsible, realistic about its own strengths and weaknesses, eager to improve, and planful about meeting new challenges.

- *Plans for improving the system.* A plan for improving your assessment system. This is different from plans to improve learning. Both will permeate your report to accreditors.

- Example of a plan to improve learning: based on assessment of students' writing, the institution will institute a writing-across-the-curriculum effort.
- Example of a plan to improve the assessment system: to gather more effective information about student writing, the assessment committee will sponsor a study of students' writing in selected general-education courses.

You will use these various forms of documentation in various ways within your self-study or report to accreditors, boards, state systems, and others. In addition to separate sections about assessment, be sure that assessment pervades your entire report or self-study. At every point, you should address these questions:

- How does the institution make decisions in this area? How do the decision makers use data about student learning?
- If an action was taken that may affect student learning, what evidence of student learning was used to make the decision?
- If plans for the future are reported, how will those plans incorporate appropriate evidence of student learning?

Example: *As one research-intensive institution began strategic planning, the institution made sure that institution-wide data were employed from the very beginning. Based on these data, the strategic plan led to general education reform, and that process, too, was informed from the beginning by data about student learning. Following is a slightly modified excerpt from their self-study report to their regional accreditor:*

The Academic Strategic Planning Committee, composed of faculty members and deans from each school, staff members, and representatives from the Board of Trustees, devoted a considerable amount of time to discussing academic challenges for undergraduate students and examining data from the graduating senior survey, the NSSE, exit surveys, the undergraduate finance and employment survey, the HEDS institution comparative data, and the faculty assessment of student portfolios. Its conclusions—that undergraduates are not intellectually challenged and do not spend enough time on their academic endeavors, that the university is losing its best and brightest students, and that the amount of time students work may be detrimental to their intellectual development—led to the recommendations put forth in Goal 1 of the Strategic Plan: "to enhance student engagement and learning through academic challenge and a rigorous intellectual environment that permeates every aspect of student life." As part of the strategic goal, the provost appointed a Task Force on General Education. That task force reviewed more recent responses to graduation surveys, exit data, and the assessment of the undergraduate writing program to help formulate its recommendations about changing the undergraduate general education curriculum. [Supporting documentation provided further details and evidence about the data and the university's actions.]

Note that the report includes several important details that you will need for your own planning and for your reports to accreditors:

- Name the decision-making bodies.
- Name the kinds of data they examined.
- Describe their conclusions.
- Tell what actions they took.

Budgeting for Assessment

Here are some factors to consider as you budget for assessment. Each of the items and decisions has been discussed earlier in this chapter, so this is just a quick list to draw together the items that may have major budgetary implications.

- Tests, surveys, and software
- Director of assessment
- More personnel in Institutional Research
- Visible resources for departments and general education initiatives

If you spend it all on the first three and have nothing left for the last one, you're out of balance.

Chapter Summary

This chapter has discussed how institutional leaders can plan and implement assessment at the institution level. After considering audiences and establishing learning goals, the institution analyzes its current assessment system and decides how to improve it.

Perhaps the single most important theme in this chapter is to make sure you are *using* the information you collect. It is better to have a small amount of data you actually use than to proliferate data you cannot use effectively. Keep it simple.

Chapter 3

For Departments and Programs

THIS CHAPTER IS aimed at those who are responsible for assessment in a department or program, whether at a community college, four-year college, or university. The chapter addresses those educators who already have well-developed assessment systems and those who are just getting started. The chapter is useful for departmental assessment, whether for regional accreditation or for specialized disciplinary accreditation in fields such as engineering, business, and health sciences. Case studies for both types are in Banta (2007a); for separately accredited disciplines, see Palomba and Banta (2001).

This chapter assumes that you have read Chapter One. Particularly important is this concept: the end of assessment is action. Assessment in the department should build on what you are already doing, help you address your real problems, enhance your students' learning, and be sustainable in terms of your time and resources. Do it to help yourselves and your students, not merely to comply with accreditors. Then, when the accreditors need to know how you are conducting assessment, you generate, as efficiently as possible, a snapshot of the sustainable, useful system you have in place.

The Basic No-Frills Departmental Assessment System

People often ask me, "What is the most basic no-frills assessment plan that is useful to the department and also acceptable to external accreditors?" Here it is.

1. Learning goals for each of your degrees, certificates, or programs of study (for example, goals for undergraduate music history, for undergraduate music performance, for your certificate in music therapy, and for each of your graduate degrees)
2. Two measures of how well your students are achieving the goals
   a. One direct measure
   My preference: A sample of student work completed at the end of their course of study, analyzed by faculty to find the strengths and weaknesses of the students as a group

For certain disciplines, a certification or licensure exam will be a second direct measure.

b. One indirect measure

My preference: Student surveys and/or focus groups asking three questions:

    i. How well did you achieve each of the following departmental learning goals? (List each department goal, with a scale for each: for example, "extremely well, very well, adequately well, not very well, not at all" or an "agree/disagree" scale)

    ii. What aspects of your education in this department helped you with your learning, and why were they helpful?

    iii. What might the department do differently that would help you learn more effectively, and why would these actions help?

In some fields, job placement rates will be important.

3. A forum to discuss data and identify action items

a. One two-hour department meeting each year, in which the department discusses whatever data it has about student learning in one of its degrees or programs, decides on one action item to improve student learning, and assigns responsibility for follow-up

b. Follow-up actions: action on one item may take several years, and that's okay; also okay to rotate degrees and programs, focusing on one or two of them each year

c. Keep minutes of the meetings for your own follow-up, and also as documentation for external audiences as needed

The basic no-frills plan is not perfect, and your department may want to expand upon it. But if every department at your institution had a useful, robust version of this plan, it would improve student learning significantly. And if every department would post, on an institutional Web site, a two- or three-page description of its assessment system for each of its degrees or programs, that Web site would be a fine tool for a regional reaccreditation review. (Chapter Two discusses the Web site in more detail.)

Basic No-Frills for Disciplinary Accreditation

Disciplinary accreditation by a disciplinary or professional organization in fields such as engineering, business, or health sciences often differs from an institution's reaccreditation by a regional accreditor. The regionals let the departments and disciplines decide on their learning goals, whereas disciplinary accreditors often dictate specific learning goals (perhaps also called "competencies," "objectives," or "outcomes") for which the department must be accountable. The department will have to map its curriculum, showing that it teaches each of the required competencies.

But do not be confused. Showing that you *teach* 150 different competencies is not the same as departmental assessment. The basic, no-frills assessment plan may still work fine. For example, engineering programs often use two measures: senior projects in which students are expected to demonstrate many of the competencies integrated into a single piece of work, plus a student survey such as those produced by Education Benchmarking, Inc. (www.webEBI.com) or a home-grown survey. Placement and retention data are also important.

The department or college meets to discuss these data and take action. (The student projects are a "direct" measure in our terms, and the survey is an "indirect" measure—but be careful, because these two terms may be used differently in different accrediting disciplines.) The challenge of disciplinary assessment is often to move from curriculum mapping for a multitude of competencies to a sufficiently simple and sustainable program assessment system.

A department that is responsible for disciplinary accreditation should concentrate on the disciplinary procedures, because they usually include and often exceed the requirements of the regional accreditors. Then, when the institution needs a report for its regional accreditor, the discipline-accredited programs can download or summarize their disciplinary assessment documents (more on reporting appears later in this chapter).

Case Studies and Examples

This section presents three case studies of departmental assessment drawn from different departments with which I have worked. None of these departments has a perfect system; all of them are developing and changing their practices, as good departments always do. The first case study illustrates the most basic, minimal assessment system; the next two cases show how departments may move in different directions to address various concerns. Shorter examples follow the case studies.

Three Case Studies of Departmental Assessment

Case 1: The Most Basic, Minimal System, Based on Oral Faculty Reports

A department of political science was very successful, very busy, with growing numbers of majors and among the highest teaching evaluations at the university. Most of the department members hated assessment and thought it was a waste of time and a plot to destroy faculty autonomy. But they had to do it.

(continued)

So, being the smart and efficient people that they were, they set about to conduct assessment in ways that would benefit their students. They decided to begin with the undergraduate major, because they did recognize that, in all the busyness, and in the struggle to build national research recognition and to attract top-quality faculty and graduate students, there was a danger that the undergraduate major would not get enough attention. They decided to institute the two-hour annual meeting on their undergraduate major.

At the first meeting, not everyone came, but those present were dedicated to ensuring that the department served its undergraduate majors effectively. No preparation had been done, and there were no rubrics (most faculty hated them or did not know what they were). But many of the faculty present were spending many hours evaluating student work, and they had ideas about what was strong and weak in the work of their students; the department could build on that faculty work. They decided to concentrate on the work of seniors, especially the research papers. So at the meeting, they went around the table systematically. Each faculty member who supervised or taught seniors named two strengths and two weaknesses that he or she observed in senior student research papers. One member kept a list on a flip chart. After everyone had named strengths and weaknesses, they discussed the list. Then they took a vote to decide on one action item. The item they chose had come up a number of times in the

faculty reports: faculty were very frustrated by the inability of senior students, as they began their senior research projects, to construct a question for inquiry in the discipline. The faculty asked the curriculum committee and the department's director of undergraduate studies (DUS) to follow up.

The DUS and the undergraduate curriculum committee decided first to examine the major's curriculum prior to the senior year, to see where the curriculum offered instruction, practice, and feedback in constructing questions for inquiry. They also administered a short, three-question survey to senior students, during one class day in the senior year, to ask seniors how well they thought they were prepared to construct questions for inquiry, what pedagogical strategies in their past courses had been most helpful, and what changes they would suggest.

Based on this information, the committee mapped those points in the present curriculum at which students received instruction, practice, and feedback in constructing questions for inquiry. The committee prepared recommendations for the department. The department acted on these recommendations, making changes to the curriculum, so as to give more instruction, practice, and feedback on constructing questions for inquiry. The following year, the department continued to implement the changes and to observe whether student skills improved. Meanwhile, they took up one of their other degree programs and began a similar assessment process. They kept minutes and records of their actions.

In this system, the reports from faculty are oral, but they are not groundless. They arise from faculty members' day-in/day-out careful examination of student work as they grade and respond to student papers. This is intensive, criterion-driven work. It results in a faculty member's sense of where students most commonly succeed or go astray. Faculty then give oral reports to the department. In the meeting, these reports are captured on a flip chart, thus creating written data or artifacts. The written lists then become the basis of departmental deliberation and action. This method of oral reporting places high trust in the accuracy of faculty grading and faculty members' ongoing knowledge of students' strengths and weaknesses, based on that grading. Methodologically, this measure has weaknesses, but there are no perfect measures available in real situations with real constraints. In most institutions, if every department were to implement this system carefully, and if the department strongly followed up with action based on faculty reports, the institution would be way ahead of where it is at present. The most important thing is that this department *acted*. This puts them ahead of a department that had better data but did not act.

A department that begins with oral reports, as this one did, may in time decide that they would benefit from a formal list of criteria or a rubric by which individual faculty, or a group of faculty readers, could more systematically evaluate senior research projects. The next example demonstrates a department that conducted its examination of student work with a rubric.

Case Study 2: A Rubric-Based Faculty Evaluation of Student Work

At a teaching institution with no graduate degrees in biology, the department had a capstone course called "Biological Research," in which students completed a major scientific research project and wrote up their work in scientific report format. To evaluate student research reports, the instructor developed a rubric (Example 2 in Appendix D). The department instituted the annual meeting. At the meeting, the capstone teacher reported students' strengths and weaknesses, using rubric scores (Table 3.1).

Table 3.1. Class Average Rubric Scores for Science Reports

Trait	Average Scores for Class in Year 1	Average Scores for Class in Year 2
Title	2.95	3.22
Introduction	3.18	3.64
Scientific Format	3.09	3.32
Methods and Materials	3.00	3.55
Non experimental Information	3.18	3.50
Designing the Experiment	2.68	3.32
Defining Operationally	2.68	3.50
Controlling Variables	2.73	3.18
Collecting Data	2.86	3.36
Interpreting Data	2.90	3.59
Overall	2.93	3.42

Source: Walvoord and Anderson, *Effective Grading: A Tool for Learning and Assessment in College,* 2nd ed., 2010, p. 167. Reprinted with permission of John Wiley and Sons, Inc.

The table allowed the department to see that, in both years, the lowest-scoring items were "Designing the Experiment" and "Controlling Variables." The department decided to focus on students' ability to design experiments, which would include the ability to control variables. A couple of faculty members formed an ad hoc committee to follow up. The committee examined the curriculum and

(continued)

talked with students in focus groups. They saw that students spent many hours in labs and read many scientific articles that represented good experimental design. But the students were not transferring those experiences into the ability to design their own experiments. Students too often approached the labs as an exercise in following the recipe and getting the right answer; they read scientific reports to find the answers to teacher-generated questions, not necessarily to learn how to design experiments themselves. The committee recommended a series of faculty brown bag lunches to discuss how to use the current labs and scientific article assignments to help students learn to design experiments

So far, the case studies have assumed a departmental meeting where everyone gathers face-to-face. But what if the department has many adjuncts? What if its faculty live and work in different locations? The next case study illustrates one way of addressing such problems.

Case Study 3: Variations of the Department Meeting

A department of English at a community college wanted to assess their literature courses, which students took as part of their associate's degree. The department had generated a list of learning goals for these courses. The course instructors were mostly adjuncts, teaching at all times of the day and night, in several different locations; any single meeting could gather only a few of them. The department had to figure out how to gather assessment information and hold a discussion among these varied faculty. So they decided to hold small, dispersed meetings, and then to bring together the results of those meetings. The department assigned its adjuncts and full-time faculty to small groups of three to four people, according to the time they could meet (for example, the Wednesday, October 12, 5 P.M. group). They asked the group to meet at a location of their own choosing for one hour. In the hour, the small group was to generate a list of two strengths and two weaknesses they saw in student work, evaluated against the written goals for the literature course. The group's "recorder" then sent in the list. A committee compiled these lists and made recommendations for departmental action.

These three case studies show how the basic no-frills plan can be adapted to many circumstances. The most important thing is to collect some reasonable data and then to take action to improve student learning. Here are more short case studies, showing the variety of measures and actions that departments and programs may employ.

Six Examples of Departmental Assessment

Several shorter examples illustrate variations for a range of situations.

1. In a department of history, faculty members examined a sample of senior student papers, and identified several common weaknesses in the students' ability to conduct historical inquiry and argument. They decided

to revise the sophomore course required of all history majors, so as to focus more effectively on these skills.

2. A department of finance designed an assignment that would test senior students' ability to think and write in ways that were important to the discipline. The assignment was administered to a senior-level finance course, and student papers were analyzed by a committee of faculty. Based on that analysis, faculty redesigned the homework assignments throughout the majors curriculum, focusing homework more intently on the skills that faculty had identified.

3. Faculty at a community college allied health program shaped a common final exam for Medical Technology, an introductory course that all their students took. Faculty met regularly to review exam results. Discussing the fact that significant numbers of students missed the exam questions that required more sophisticated understanding, faculty wondered whether exam performance was linked to reading skills. Subsequent investigation indeed showed a relationship. The faculty took several steps, including giving students clearer information about the importance of reading skills and the reading resources available to them; asking experienced students to talk to new students about study time and study methods necessary for the program; and increasing the support and faculty development for instructors, many of whom were adjuncts.

4. A department of theology began offering online graduate courses. They constructed a questionnaire to be completed by each student. Many students suggested improving the way online discussion boards were managed. The department brought in an experienced teacher of online graduate courses to hold a workshop about how to make online discussion boards more effective for learning. Then the department looked to see whether student comments about the discussion boards became more favorable.

5. A school of business conducted online Executive MBA degree programs at a distant site. Annually, the director of the MBA program and several of the key instructors traveled to the distant site and hosted a dinner to which all the students at that site were invited. At the dinner, in addition to regular social interaction, a time was set aside for the participants at each table of six to discuss a series of questions about the program. A facilitator at each table took notes about strengths and weaknesses of the program from the students' point of view. These notes were compiled into a report, which became the basis for further improvements to the program.

6. A community college dental hygiene program regularly administered surveys to its students. One year, the students seemed unusually dissatisfied. Several of them came to the program chair in person, as well. The department asked the director of the teaching excellence center to facilitate a meeting of the students, at which no dental hygiene faculty would be present. The facilitator framed the meeting so as to focus on aspects that were or were not effective for students' learning. Students voiced their frustration with certain organizational and logistical aspects of the program they thought were interfering with their learning. The facilitator took notes, checked her understanding with the students, and then later submitted a written report to the department about the students' complaints and suggestions. The department then acted to address the issues.

Further details about the first three examples can be found in Walvoord and Anderson (2010). More case studies appear in Banta, Jones, and Black (2009), Palomba and Banta (2001), Banta (2007a), and in the pages of *Assessment Update* (www3.interscience.wiley.com).

Guidelines for Departmental Assessment

Doing It Now!

No matter how inadequate you think your data are, put the annual meeting in place *now*, without waiting for the perfect data. Choose an action item based on the data you have. Then, if needed, take steps to gather better data.

Involving Adjunct Faculty

Creating a forum for discussion is challenging when a large proportion of the instructors in a particular program or general education curriculum are adjuncts. Here are some actions you might take:

• Ask adjuncts to submit, along with their grades, a short report of students' strengths and weaknesses measured against departmental or general education learning goals. Use these reports, along with those of full-time faculty, as data for discussion. Even if adjuncts are not otherwise involved in the discussion, keep them informed about how their classroom data were analyzed and acted upon.

• To include adjuncts in the discussion of assessment data, hold several small meetings instead of one large meeting, as in the case study of the community college earlier in this chapter. Alternately, adjuncts or full-time faculty who live or teach at distant sites can participate in discussion by the same technology used for online learning or conference calls.

Preparing Data for the Department Meeting

To achieve maximum effectiveness for the meeting, whether of a committee or of the entire department or program, it may be helpful to organize the data ahead of time. Case Study 2 (biology) discussed earlier showed a table of rubric scores that had been prepared ahead of time (Table 3.1). A wider array of data was organized by a department of economics, whose data consisted of (1) faculty analysis of student senior projects (done with a list of learning goals but not a formal rubric); (2) focus groups of students; and (3) an alumni survey, asking alumni two questions: first, which of the department's learning goals the alumni thought were most important to them in their careers, and second, how well they believed they had achieved those goals during their course of study in the major. Exhibit 3.1 shows how data from these three sources might be prepared, prior to the department meeting, so that faculty can more easily analyze the data and take action.

EXHIBIT 3.1

Organization of Assessment Data for Departmental Discussion

Department: Economics

Measures

- *Analysis of the senior capstone research projects* (written papers plus oral presentations). Three faculty examined a sample of written papers and attended oral presentations for a sample of senior students. These faculty produced written analyses of the student work, using the learning goals as criteria. These analyses were submitted to the assistant chair.

- *Focus groups of current students*, who met for an hour with the assistant chair.

- *Alumni Survey*, conducted by the department under the leadership of the assistant chair, asking alumni to

  - Rate how important each of the learning goals were to them in their careers. 5 = essential;

4 = very important; 3 = important; 2 = slightly important; 1 = not important. The ratings were averaged to produce scores for the group as a whole.

- Rank how well they had achieved this goal during their major. Respondents were to arrange all seven learning goals in ranked order, giving a 7 to the highest and a 1 to the lowest. These rankings were averaged to produce a ranking for the group as a whole: 7th = highest; 1st = lowest.

Goals, Assessment Methods, and Findings

Goal: Critical thinking (analytical) and communication skills, to enable undergraduate students to think and communicate like economists (in other words, to become skilled in the logic and rhetoric of economics)

(continued)

Subgoals/ Objectives	Alumni Survey: Importance 5 = Essential; 1 = not important	Alumni Survey: Achievement (7 = highest)	Analysis of Capstone Student Projects	Focus Groups of Current Students
A. Mathematical Methods: To use mathematical methods to represent economic concepts and to analyze economic issues	4.33. Very important	2nd of 7 objectives. Low	None included math.	Amount of math varies among classes. Maybe calculus should be required.
B. Theoretical Models: To represent economic relationships in terms of theoretical models	4.33. Very important	3rd of 7 objectives. Low	Models used in papers and presentations with reasonable success	Achievement is enhanced by having TA sessions. Theory course is good foundation if taken before other courses.
C. Gather Data: To gather economic data pertinent to economic theories in order to analyze economic questions	4.17. Very important	5th of 7 objectives. High	Students showed an ability to collect data but over-relied on the Web.	Library research used in a few classes only.
D. Statistics: To use statistical methods to analyze economic questions	3.83. Very important	6th of 7 objectives. High	Little evidence of statistical methods	Limited exposure. Complaint about book used.
E. Software: To use statistical computer software to analyze economic issues	3.33. Important	7th of 7 objectives. Highest	Little evidence of use	Concern that software used in career will be different.
F. Writing: To express economic ideas succinctly and professionally in writing	4.17. Very important	4th of 7 objectives. Medium	Writing skills of students generally acceptable, but not "very good" or "excellent"	Writing is required more than speaking. In particular, research papers are required in 400 and 426.
G. Oral: To express economic ideas succinctly and professionally	4.5. Very important/ essential	1st of 7 objectives. Lowest	Presentations revealed a lack of training in how to present as well as nervousness.	Most courses do not involve oral communication, although it would be useful after graduation in the workforce. One idea was a sequence of courses in communication as part of the Arts and Sciences college requirements. More discussion and presentations were advised.

Choosing the Action Issue

Once the data have been organized in a fashion similar to Table 3.1 or Exhibit 3.1, the next step is for a committee, a chair, or the department as a whole to interpret, prioritize, and decide upon a sustainable, reasonable course of action to improve student learning. For this further analysis and prioritizing, you can combine three considerations:

Question 1: *What is most important?* The faculty themselves might determine what is most important, or they might rely on alumni responses, as did the economics department. The economics department might examine Exhibit 3.1, asking, "Which subgoal had the highest importance to alumni in their careers after graduation?" (Answer: Oral communication)

Question 2: *Which areas show the greatest problems with learning?* In Exhibit 3.1, the economics department could ask, "Which subgoal had the lowest score in terms of how well alumni thought they achieved the goal?" (Answer: Oral communication)

From the data in Exhibit 3.1, alumni seem to be saying that oral communication is very important, but that they did not achieve it very well. In the right-hand columns of the exhibit, the faculty analysis of students' oral reports shows problems with oral reports, and students themselves report problems. Thus, oral communication seems a significant candidate for departmental attention.

Question 3: *What is feasible?* Given this analysis, an obvious action item for the department is to try to improve students' learning in oral communication. However, the department may decide that this problem cannot be successfully addressed at this point in the department's history. It's okay to select a problem the department thinks it can successfully address. For example, in the data from Exhibit 3.1, the use of mathematical methods is rated very important by alumni and is fairly low in alumni achievement. Mathematical methods do not appear in the capstone project, and student focus groups report inconsistent use. The department might choose this issue instead of the oral communication issue for their current efforts.

Gathering Further Information

Once the department or general education group has chosen an item for action, the next question is whether additional information might be needed before the group knows what actions to take. Suppose the economics department chooses the oral communication item. It might need to know, for example, what alumni consider to be the most valuable types of oral communication—the ability to make a presentation to an external audience? To talk persuasively with clients? To participate in a discussion with colleagues? What does the research literature say about how students learn oral communication? Are there models of good practice in other departments or institutions? Where in the current curriculum are students receiving instruction, practice, and feedback about oral communication? What do students believe would be the most helpful way to learn oral communication skills? If students were to be required to take a speech course, is there one that would meet their needs? Would the communications department be willing to offer such a course?

Taking Action

Once the needed information has been gathered, the next step is to propose action(s) that seem likely to enhance student learning and that are feasible given the department's resources. Suggested actions might include requiring majors to take a speech course and identifying courses with their own curriculum that will offer practice and feedback in oral communication. Establish responsibility and a timeline for completing these actions. Then follow up. It may take several years for a single action item to be addressed. That's okay; you don't need a new action initiative each year.

You should keep good records of the meeting itself and of the follow-up actions, both for your own internal use and for reports you may have to submit.

Evaluating Action

Once you've taken action, it is sensible to ask whether your actions have achieved increased student learning. For example, once the curricular changes for biology or economics have been in place for a while, the department may examine the capstone projects of students who have experienced the revised curriculum. Follow-up to check the efficacy of the action is often a multiyear project. In the meantime, other variables may intervene: the department's students change; other curricular changes are made; faculty change; leadership changes; budget cuts make everything harder. It's not an experimental design in which one can control all the variables. It's an ongoing process in which the responsible department that cares about student learning takes the time to look carefully at the best evidence they have, takes an action that seems liable to enhance the learning, and then, as possible, tries to check whether the action has had its intended result. Tobias (1992) studied science departments that were exceptionally successful in preparing undergraduates. The secret of their success was not their adoption of innovative methods, but their *consistent, steady attention and action*. Good assessment is paying attention.

Section Summary	
• Construct assessment that you can use to improve student learning and that is sustainable in terms of time and resources. • The basic no-frills plan can work well, provided that you *act* on your assessment data.	• Start *now* with an annual department meeting to examine whatever data you have. • Prepare data carefully for departmental discussion. • Choose your action item based on what is most important, most problematic, and feasible.

Special Circumstances for Assessment

So far, the examples have primarily been taken from undergraduate majors in fairly traditional institutions. What about the department's general education courses? Two-year degrees in community colleges? Multidisciplinary programs? Graduate programs? Online programs? This section addresses each of those particular circumstances. The same basic strategies apply: articulate goals for student learning; gather information about how well students are achieving the goals; use the information for action.

General Education

One of the suggestions made in Chapter Four, on general education assessment, is that each department be responsible for assessing student learning and taking action to improve learning in the general education courses the department offers. Then these departmental findings and actions can be aggregated and synthesized to suggest action at the institutional level.

Suppose that, the year following its meeting about the undergraduate majors, the economics department focused on analyzing student work in its general education courses, using a similar process. The process would begin as the institution, through its general education committee or faculty senate, defined general education goals. Perhaps the institution-wide body would state only broad goals such as "Students will think critically" or "write effectively to a variety of audiences." Or perhaps the institution would suggest or require that general education courses adhere to more specific goals ("Students will write an argument in which they state a position on a debatable issue, support their position with evidence, and address counter-arguments"). Certainly, the department would have to fashion more specific goals and criteria for particular assignments within its general education courses. Thus, fashioning explicit goals tied to general education goals is the first step.

To gather information about how well students are meeting the gen ed goals, the department might use the same measures as the basic, no-frills plan described earlier—one direct measure, one indirect measure, and an annual meeting to analyze the data and identify an action item. For the direct measure, the department might ask a group of readers to examine a sample of student work from its gen ed courses, and/or ask instructors to submit reports of students' strengths and weaknesses (these options are discussed in Chapter One). For the indirect measure, the department might administer a survey to students in its general education courses. Prior to the department meeting, someone would organize the data in much the same way as Table 3.1 or Exhibit 3.1. After deliberation by the department as a whole and/or by faculty involved in the gen ed courses, the department or faculty might take an action aimed at addressing a problem or building on a strength.

In some institutions, departments are asked to assess general education skills within all their majors. The assessment often focuses on a capstone course or a course near the end of the students' program. The economics department discussed earlier was not specifically asked to do this, but they nonetheless generated measures of oral and written communication, as well as quantitative reasoning and critical thinking, as part of what they wanted from their majors. Once the department had assessed these learning goals within its capstone students, it might send a report to the general education committee, outlining the department's findings and actions on these general education goals. The general education committee would combine these departmental reports and identify common themes or problems that needed to be addressed at a level larger than a single department. For example, oral communication might emerge as a problem in a number of disciplinary capstone courses, in which case the general education program might focus on helping students across the curriculum to gain more instruction, feedback, and practice in oral communication.

Two-Year Degrees or Certificates

A department or program can evaluate a two-year degree or certificate using a version of the same basic no-frills plan. Faculty can evaluate students' work at the end of the degree or certificate program. The faculty can sit down annually for an assessment meeting and consider those evaluations, together with other data such as student job placement, student or alumni surveys, employer feedback, or student pass rates for licensure exams.

In addition to certificate programs, the community college may have an associate's degree for students who intend to transfer into a four-year program at another institution. The community college needs a set of learning goals for these students. There will be two difficulties in measuring how well students are achieving the goals: (1) students may take their courses in no specific sequence, so it is impossible to tell whether a particular course appears early or late in the student's course of study; and (2) courses for the associate's degree are offered not by one department, but by many.

To overcome the first difficulty—students take courses in many sequences—the college has several options. One option is to analyze student work in a particular course or courses, regardless of how many courses each student may have taken. That strategy will reveal how well students in a given course or courses are able to write or think critically or use quantitative reasoning. Another option is to analyze a sample of student work only from those students who have already taken a certain number of credits or who have already taken certain other courses such as the required writing course. That strategy will reveal how well students near the end of their studies are able to write or think critically.

To overcome the second difficulty—associate's degree courses are offered by many departments—the college needs to create a forum for faculty discussion and action that includes members or representatives from the various departments that offer courses within the associate's degree. That faculty group needs to consider evidence from students' classroom work as well as data such as students' success in their subsequent four-year degree programs, student and alumni surveys, retention, and standardized tests. The forum of multidisciplinary faculty must work with departments to act on the findings.

> Example: *To assess learning in its associate's degree, Isothermal Community College involved 100 percent of its full-time faculty to identify competencies, develop rubrics, evaluate student work, and take action (Womack, 2007). They established multiple cross-disciplinary committees to evaluate student work for general education competencies. All faculty were asked to sign up for one of the committees. Campuswide report meetings facilitated communication among the committees. The Assessment Task Force then encouraged faculty to weave general education competencies into all their courses. They constructed curriculum maps showing the courses where general education competencies were being addressed. The task force offered faculty development to support these initiatives. Finally, after all these cross-cutting avenues of communication and collaboration were in place, the college asked each program to develop an assessment model in which the program assessed not only its own disciplinary learning but also the general education competencies.*

Other community college case studies can be found in Banta (2004), Banta, Jones, and Black (2009), and Serban and Friedlander (2004).

Multidisciplinary Programs

Multidisciplinary or interdisciplinary programs face similar problems, in that they must create a multidisciplinary faculty forum to analyze assessment data and make recommendations. Interdisciplinary programs, concentrations, and similar programs often have a common capstone, which offers a perfect place to collect student work. Even if students' capstone projects are quite diverse because students have followed different pathways through the multidisciplinary curriculum, faculty overseeing the program should be able to assess student strengths and weaknesses in terms of broad goals such as critical thinking, data analysis, or use of sources. Based on the analysis, the interdisciplinary program must take action. Its options for action may be limited if it does not hire its own faculty or even determine which courses its various departmental contributors will offer, but within these constraints, the interdisciplinary program may negotiate with contributing departments, change its capstone or its introductory course, offer faculty development, or other actions.

Graduate Programs

Graduate programs may be the easiest to assess. Typically, students are asked to conduct a research project, take a comprehensive exam, write a thesis, or complete a field placement that asks them to pull together what they have learned. Often, multiple faculty members in the department are involved in supervising and evaluating these student works. What is needed then is to convene a forum of the graduate faculty to formally and systematically consider the strengths and weaknesses of student work as a whole and to take action as needed.

Example: *A department of sociology examined its students' comprehensive exams and dissertations as well as their conference presentations and publications. The graduate school conducted exit exams with graduate students from all disciplines, trying to capture information from those who dropped out as well as those who completed the degree. In its annual meeting, the graduate faculty each presented a list of strengths and weaknesses they found in working with students' exams and dissertations. They made a common list. They also analyzed the exit interview data. Their action item was to try to increase the number of publications their graduate students produced. They talked with graduate students about strategies and decided to introduce a one-credit seminar on publication that was voluntary for the pilot year and subsequently was required for all their doctoral candidates. The number of publications rose significantly.*

Additional case studies about graduate programs may be found in Banta, Jones, and Black (2009).

Online Education

In assessing online education, the data will be the same, but probably collected online: student work and online student surveys, interviews or focus groups. The questions and discussion will be similar: "How well are our students learning, and what factors are influencing their learning?" But because the teaching methods and the media of communication are different, the actions may be different.

Example: *Faculty in one graduate program that was aimed at working adults observed that the students, in their written papers, relied heavily upon personal experiences but had trouble interpreting those experiences in terms of theoretical frameworks. Most of the courses in the program required students to contribute to online discussions, but faculty observed that the online discussions seemed to elicit many personal "war stories" but not enough discussion of the theoretical frameworks. So the department held a workshop for its online faculty on how to shape and guide online discussions to elicit thoughtful application of theoretical frames.*

Reporting Departmental Assessment

When you report your departmental assessment to audiences outside the department, you are likely to include four topics that are common to all audiences and a final topic that will differ depending on the audience. Exhibit 3.2 illustrates all the topics:

- Three common topics:
  1. Departmental learning goals
  2. Measures of student learning: a description of the ongoing system by which the department uses assessment information for action
  3. Reflections or recommendations about the quality of the data or the system

- Final topic for accreditors and others who need to know that the department is doing assessment. This topic gives examples of how the department has used assessment information for action. It answers the question, "Does this department regularly use assessment information for action?"
- Alternate final topic for program review, budgeting, strategic planning, and any audience that needs to know *what* the department has discovered, what actions it plans to take, and what resources it needs. This topic discusses the most recent assessment data, the department's planned actions, and the resources needed to implement the plans.

EXHIBIT 3.2

Departmental Assessment Report

Author Note: This is a biology department report for its undergraduate majors. Similar reports would be produced for certificate and graduate programs in the department.

Section 1: Learning Goals for Majors

1. Describe and apply basic biological information and concepts.
2. Conduct original biological research and report results orally and in writing to scientific audiences.
3. Apply ethical principles of the discipline in regard to human and animal subjects, environmental protection, use of sources, and collaboration with colleagues.

Web site and/or other avenues by which these are readily available to students, prospective students, and faculty:

Section 2: Measures and Use of Information

Measures	Goal 1	Goal 2	Goal 3	Use of the Information
Standardized test given to all seniors AND Final exams of three basic biology courses required of all majors	X			Data are reported to the department annually by the standardized exam committee and the instructors of the three basic courses. The department supports and encourages the instructors, takes any appropriate department-level actions, and reports meeting outcomes to dean or other body which has resources to address problems, and to those composing reports for accreditation or other external audiences. All data are reviewed as part of program review every seven years.

Measures	Goal 1	Goal 2	Goal 3	Use of the Information
In senior capstone course, students complete an original scientific experiment, write it up in scientific report format, and also make an oral report to the class. The instructor(s) use a rubric to evaluate student work.	X	X	X	Senior capstone instructor(s) share students' rubric scores with the department. The department takes action as above. Program review as above.
Alumni survey asks how well alumni/alumnae thought they learned to conduct and communicate scientific research, what aspects of the program helped them learn, and what suggestions they have for improvement in the program.	X	X	X	Data reviewed by department for action, as above. Program review as above.
Sample of regional employers gathered two years ago to reflect how well our majors are doing and give advice to department.	X	X	X	Data reviewed annually by department for action, as above.

Section 3: Recommendations for Improving Assessment Processes

The standardized national test is costly and time consuming to administer, has low student motivation in its current format, and its results are difficult to map to our curriculum. Committee should review usefulness of the national test.

Alternate Final Section 4: For Accreditation: Examples of Action Based on Assessment Data

Author Note: This final section of the report is for audiences, such as accreditors, who need to know *that* the department regularly uses assessment results for action.

- Two years ago, our advisory council of regional employers recommended that our majors had a good level of biological knowledge but needed stronger skills in actually conducting biological research. Data from the alumni survey also mentioned this problem. We instituted the required capstone course, which requires students to conduct original scientific research, and we asked the instructor(s) annually to report to the department on student research and communication skills demonstrated by their capstone projects. In three years, when several cohorts of majors have passed through the capstone, we will again survey alumni and employers to see whether student skills have increased, and we will review data from all years of the capstone projects.

- The capstone instructor(s) last year reported low graphing skills in seniors; we arranged with the mathematics department for greater emphasis on graphing and better assessment of graphing in the required math course. The capstone instructor(s) will report next year whether graphing skills are stronger. Prof. Brody is currently developing a rubric to assess graphing skills more systematically in the capstone.

Alternate Final Section 4: For Budgeting and Planning

Author Note: If the assessment report is part of program review, planning, or budgeting cycles, the list of examples in Section 4 above would be replaced by current findings, actions, and budget requests. Chapter Two discusses these documents in more detail, including an outline for program review.

Current Findings: Analysis of student senior capstone work, as well as senior student surveys reveal that many students are weak in graphing skills. Particularly, students choose randomly among types of graphics, rather than selecting the best for the audience and purpose; they do not provide enough information on the graph itself alone; they draw the graphics in misleading ways; they do not correctly title the graphs or label the axes of the graphs; and they do not integrate the graphic information appropriately into the text. The department would like to address this problem as its action item.

Action Plan: The department has appointed a task force to take these actions:

- Search for, or construct, a diagnostic test of graphic competency that could be given to students to pinpoint their strengths and weaknesses in graphing.
- Investigate online, interactive graphics instruction modules that might be integrated into the curriculum.
- Identify courses in which more graphic instruction, practice, feedback, and assessment could be included.
- Discuss with the mathematics department how the required math courses might better provide our students with the graphic skills they need.

Resources

- Summer stipend for two professors to complete the first two items above
- If necessary, purchase or license fees for the test or modules in the first two items above
- Pizza lunch for faculty to discuss classroom strategies for helping students with graphics

Chapter Summary

This chapter has emphasized that assessment in the department or program can be sensible, sustainable, and useful for student learning. Building on what you already have, using the basic no-frills system as a reference point, gather data that shows the strengths and weaknesses of student work in the program. You need reasonable data but not the world's most perfect research design.

You are looking for something to act on. Don't try to fix everything at once. Keep it small, start with a pilot, keep it simple. There's no need to cram at the last minute for accreditation reviews; just implement a sensible, sustainable system, and then, when the accreditors or others need to know what you're doing, take a snapshot of the system you have in place.

Chapter 4

For General Education

GENERAL EDUCATION GOALS may be the same as institution-wide goals, and they may be assessed not only within the general education curriculum but also within the major, in student affairs, and in other areas. This kind of useful integration is addressed in Chapter Two, which shows how to construct an institution-wide system of assessment around goals that are being addressed in many areas.

This chapter, however, is more narrowly addressed to the general education *curricular requirements*, including specific required courses such as composition or math, courses used to fulfill distribution requirements, and special programs such as learning communities or first-year experiences. In community colleges, general education may include not only courses required of all students, but all the courses required for the associate's degree that is intended to prepare students for transfer to a four-year institution. This chapter guides those who are responsible for addressing the question, "How well does our general education curriculum work to help our students achieve the goals of the college or university?" This chapter assumes that you have read Chapter One, about the basics of assessment.

The first section of the chapter explores how to establish a vision, clear committee responsibilities, audiences and purposes, and goals for student learning at several levels. The next section presents the basic no-frills general education assessment system. The third section offers guidelines for making decisions about your general education system. The final section suggests how to report general education assessment to external audiences such as accreditors.

Establish Vision, Responsibilities, Audiences, and Goals

Establish a Guiding Vision

In every communication and every action, you want to communicate the vision that drives general education assessment:

- We are an institution that cares about students' learning in general education.
- We want to know whether students are achieving the learning we want for them.

- We want to take action based on that information.
- We want to use assessment to help us make most efficient use of our resources.
- We want to meet accreditors' requirements, but our central goal is to improve student learning.

Define Your Responsibilities

Chapter Two discussed the institution-wide system of assessment within which general education assessment operates. If you are an assessment or general education director or committee, be clear about your relationship to the rest of the "digestion" of the assessment system (Exhibit 2.1). In particular, be sure to clarify whether you are responsible for

- Supporting and improving assessment *processes* for the general education curriculum
- Reviewing assessment *data* on student learning and recommending improvements in curriculum, pedagogy, or related factors intended to improve learning in the general education courses

Define Your Audiences and Purposes

Next, identify all potential audiences and purposes for general education assessment. Though an accrediting body may be the first audience, assessment data may have other audiences as well: recruitment, fund-raising, new student orientation, and so on. The most important audience is the institution itself; assessment must help it enhance student learning. Appendix C will help you identify potential audiences and purposes for your work.

Articulate General Education Goals

Constructing Broad Goals

The basis for assessing learning in general education is to articulate the broad learning goals for the general education curriculum as a whole. These broad-level goals may simply adopt some of the institutional goals such as critical thinking or writing. Check that your goals address the guidelines of your accreditor or your state system. Sometimes these guidelines require that, for example, you include "information literacy" among the gen ed goals or that you adhere to statewide goals intended to facilitate students' transfer among state institutions.

Constructing Specific Goals

In addition to the broad general education goals, you will need more specific goals. You can construct these specific goals centrally or you can allow individual programs to construct their own versions of the broad goals, letting faculty in these settings work out their own ideas and language. Here is an example of each approach.

Option 1. Require the same specific goals for all general education courses. This option ensures unanimity, encourages faculty collaboration, and facilitates cross-disciplinary sharing of general education data.

> Example: *In one institution, the general education committee, working closely from the institution's learning goals, constructed a set of general education goals, including critical thinking, writing, and so on. These were passed by the faculty senate as the basis for general education. Every course that counted for general education credit would be expected to address at least one of these broad general education goals. Then the general education committee formed faculty committees which generated more specific goals (or objectives) for each of the general goals. For example, under critical thinking, the relevant committee generated the following objectives that every general education course that claimed to address critical thinking would have to adopt:*
>
> - *Analyze, construct, and critically evaluate various types of critical thinking processes such as arguments; solutions to problems; or analyses of texts, situations, and structures*
> - *Appropriately find, use, and cite sources as needed*
> - *Identify logical fallacies and bias in one's own and others' thinking*
> - *Address counter-arguments, counter-evidence, and alternative points of view*

Centrally generating specific goals can lead to curricular coherence and a clear message to everyone about what "critical thinking" means at this institution. The disadvantage is that disciplinary differences in a concept such as "critical thinking" may be constrained. For example, the four specific goals above were heavily influenced by the philosophers on the committee; chemists or sociologists might define critical thinking somewhat differently.

Option 2: Allow individual programs to establish their own specific goals. An alternative is to allow individual departments, programs, or even courses to construct their own specific goals under the centrally determined broad goals. This option allows greatest program and faculty autonomy, encourages local buy-in, and makes it easier for faculty to construct assignments and assessment criteria that reflect their own disciplinary languages.

Example: *One institution had "Communicate effectively in writing" as an institution-wide goal. The general education committee adopted that goal as a general education goal. The committee asked each general education course or program that claimed to address written communication to develop its own more specific goals. Here is a selection of the goals the composition program developed for the required gen ed composition course.*

- *Construct logical and coherent arguments, recognizing the role and value of credibility (ethos), point of view, emotional appeals (pathos), and individual voice and style in writing and in speaking,*
- *Employ syntax, usage, and style appropriate for academic disciplines, for professional environments, and for personal expression and interpersonal exchange,*
- *Describe, summarize, and analyze written and spoken discourse, noting how language affects and reflects our perception of human values, cultural perspectives, and gender identities.*

Because the composition faculty had participated in shaping these goals, they were willing to ensure that these goals were central to all composition sections. When they conducted assessment of the composition program, they translated these goals into specific criteria by which to evaluate student classroom work.

Other programs and courses could establish their own versions of the writing goal. For example, when the institution launched a system of "writing intensive" courses in the disciplines, the leaders of that initiative formulated a somewhat different set of subgoals under "Communicate effectively in writing." For writing-intensive courses, students will be able to

- *Communicate in writing about subjects within the discipline, following disciplinary conventions for effective inquiry, reasoning, and expression*
- *Shape disciplinary writing to the needs of various audiences*
- *Follow useful processes for planning, researching, drafting, revising, and editing their writing*
- *Use Edited Standard Written English (ESWE) conventions in their formal, finished writing*
- *Use writing effectively for themselves as a mode of discovery, exploration, and inquiry*

In addition to the learning goals, the committee also developed guidelines for how to conduct a writing-intensive (W-I) course—for example, W-I courses would require at least twenty-four pages of finished writing; instructors would offer explicit instruction about writing in the discipline; instructors would arrange for draft response on at least one piece of writing; and instructors would base at least 25 percent of the final course grade on the qualities of students' writing. Such pedagogical guidelines are important, but it's equally important to shape learning goals. In this instance, the W-I goals and guidelines were passed by the faculty senate and became the basis for accepting courses as "writing intensive."

The point is that specific general education goals may be formulated centrally or left to individual programs and faculty. You should choose the option that best fits your institutional culture.

Section Summary	
• Establish a vision. Define your responsibilities carefully and clarify your audiences and purposes.	• Establish broad general education goals. Then choose whether to construct more specific goals centrally or within individual disciplines and courses.

The Basic No-Frills System

Once your learning goals, both general and specific, are in place, you need two other components of an assessment system: measures of how well your students are achieving the goals and a structure for taking action based on that information.

This section presents a basic no-frills system for those two components. The no-frills system, in my view, would not contain a standardized tests or an institution-wide portfolio system. Both can be useful, but they are expensive, time consuming, and difficult to implement, for reasons discussed in Chapter One. Instead, my basic no-frills system uses departments and programs to collect data from their own general education courses and make changes there. This is a powerful feedback loop, as departments invest in their own data, their own analysis, and their own actions. The department's analysis of its data, its actions based on those data, and its recommendations for action at higher levels are then reported to a central body or person, who aggregates the findings for institution-wide analysis and action. Thus you are still gathering student work institution-wide, but that work is first gathered and analyzed and used at the department level, and then summarized and used for action at higher levels.

One institution-wide measure I include in the basic no-frills system is an institution-wide student survey, because I have seen institutions use such surveys for meaningful action. The Web site of one such survey, the National Survey of Student Engagement, contains valuable resources about using survey results for campus change (www.nsse.iub.edu).

More complex systems beyond the no-frills may include more data, such as national standardized tests or institution-wide portfolios. However, no matter how much data you have, you still must have a system for digesting and using those data. You still must spur meaningful involvement and action at the levels of the department, program, and classroom.

The basic no-frills system includes

1. A requirement that every department or unit that offers general education courses take responsibility for assessing student learning in its gen ed courses, including
   - Course learning goals consonant with the gen ed goals
   - Course assignments and tests that address those goals
   - Information about student achievement of the goals
     - Analysis of a sample of student work
     - Student survey, interviews, or focus groups
   - A system for using the assessment information at the department level for improvement
2. A periodic two-page report from the department to the assessment or general education committee telling
   - What the department has identified as areas of strength and areas of concern in student achievement of the relevant goals
   - What actions the department is taking
   - What issues the department believes should be addressed at the institutional level
3. An institution-wide student survey such as the National Survey of Student Engagement (NSSE, pronounced "Nessie") or its companions for other types of institutions, including the Community College Survey of Student Engagement (CCSSE, pronounced "Sessie"), both of which can be found at www.nsse.iub.edu (see Chapter Two for a discussion of surveys)

4. A body or committee that examines the two-page departmental reports and the student survey data and makes recommendations for action, (part of "digestion" described in Chapter Two)

5. Decision makers at every level who take the recommendations seriously and act on them

Figure 4.1 illustrates a general education assessment system with these basic no-frills components, as well as some additional data. Read the diagram in conjunction with the larger institution-wide system illustrated in Figure 2.2. Both figures should be read from the bottom up, starting with the sources of assessment data in the lowest row of boxes. Then follow the arrows, which represent the flow of data, into processes that aggregate, analyze, and disseminate the data (what I call

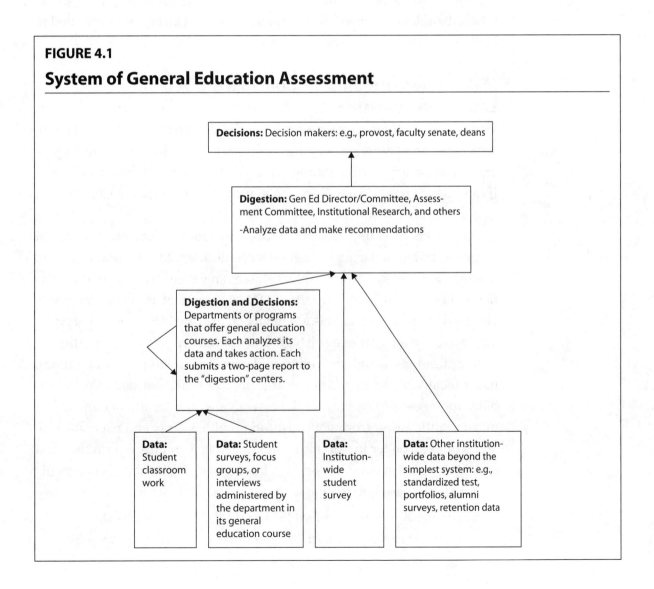

FIGURE 4.1

System of General Education Assessment

Decisions: Decision makers: e.g., provost, faculty senate, deans

Digestion: Gen Ed Director/Committee, Assessment Committee, Institutional Research, and others

-Analyze data and make recommendations

Digestion and Decisions: Departments or programs that offer general education courses. Each analyzes its data and takes action. Each submits a two-page report to the "digestion" centers.

Data: Student classroom work

Data: Student surveys, focus groups, or interviews administered by the department in its general education course

Data: Institution-wide student survey

Data: Other institution-wide data beyond the simplest system: e.g., standardized test, portfolios, alumni surveys, retention data "digestion"), and then to centers of decision making that can act on the information. The basic no-frills system would use only three of the data boxes: classroom work, student responses within the department, and a national student survey. An expanded system would employ other data as well. But do not add standardized tests or institution-wide portfolios unless you will gain enough additional information to make it worth the considerable cost.

Guidelines for General Education Assessment

This section offers guidelines as you shape your general education assessment system, whether it is no-frills or more complex. The guidelines emphasize making departments and programs responsible for assessing their own general education courses, and establishing avenues by which their data, analyses, and recommendations can be communicated to higher-level decision makers.

Making Departments Responsible for General Education Assessment

When general education courses are housed within an independent program, such as the first-year composition program or the learning communities program, that program will naturally focus on its general education offerings. It can operate much like a department, using the strategies in Chapter 3 to assess its students' learning.

However, assessing general education courses that are housed in degree-granting departments can be more difficult. In my view, however, making departments responsible for assessing their own general education courses is critically important. The department is where money is allocated, course assignments are made, faculty are hired and supervised. You can spend lots of money on high-cost assessment software, e-portfolios, standardized tests, and institution-wide surveys of students and alumni, but if faculty in the departments and programs are not taking responsibility for assessing learning in their own general education courses, you may see little result from your institution-wide efforts and expenditures. You would do better to skip the standardized test and the e-portfolios and spend the same money supporting the improvements that departments want to make based on their assessment.

Example: *A provost examined the results of the institution's standardized test of students' writing and critical reasoning, together with the institution's NSSE results. There were a couple of clear problem areas, including critical thinking and writing. The provost gathered together the department chairs and shared these data with them. They wouldn't bite. They criticized the methodology and decided that the data could not be trusted. There was no system in place to make departments responsible for assessing their own general education courses, so faculty found it easy to shrug off responsibility for the unfamiliar standardized tests and surveys. There was no system by which faculty were gathering student work from general education courses and analyzing students' critical thinking and writing for themselves—an analysis that might have been used to confirm or disconfirm the results of the standardized test. There was no system by which departments administered student surveys or met with student focus groups in their own general education courses, so there was no immediate experience of students' voices to augment the institution-wide survey.*

What would a department-level general education assessment system look like? Basically, the department gathers, analyzes, and acts on data from its general education offerings, much as it does for its majors or certificate students (Chapter Three), except that instead of analyzing a student's course of study for a degree, the department or program is analyzing the individual courses students take as part of their general education. If the department offers courses that are taken by both majors or certificate students and also by students fulfilling their general education requirement, then the department must analyze the learning of the general education students in light of the general education goals.

Example: *The history department teaches a number of courses that are taken by students fulfilling a general education requirement, as well as by majors or prospective majors. The department begins by developing learning goals for its general education students, based on institution-wide general education goals. It asks each of its faculty teaching a course that can count for general education to state, in the syllabus, the general education goals the course will address.*

Next, the department establishes an annual two-hour "gen ed assessment" meeting. All faculty teaching or administering history courses are invited to the meeting. Adjuncts are offered additional compensation to participate, and every attempt is made to arrange the meeting time so that the largest possible number of instructors, including regular, adjunct, and graduate teaching assistants, can attend. At this meeting, the department considers any data it has about student learning in its gen ed courses. These data may include

- *A sample of essays written for history courses by students who are taking the course for gen ed credit (as Chapter One suggests, the department can ask individual faculty to analyze their own students' papers and identify strengths and weaknesses, or a group of faculty can analyze a sample of papers drawn from multiple classes)*

- *A survey administered to gen ed students in all the sections, asking them how well they thought they achieved the learning goals of the gen ed course, what aspects of the course best helped them do so, and what suggestions they have for improvement (focus groups or interviews could also be used, addressing the same questions)*

- *Relevant items from the institution-wide student survey, institution-wide standardized tests, or other institution-wide data*

At the meeting, the department discusses the data and identifies one *item to work on. That one item may require further information gathering about the nature of the problem and/or the factors that might be affecting it. For example, suppose the department decides to try to improve the way students address counter-arguments as they write their argumentative essays on historical issues. The department might examine faculty members' own experience and the research literature to find out whether some pedagogical strategies are more effective than others for teaching students to address counter-arguments; the department might talk with colleagues in the writing program to find out whether students manage counter-argument effectively in writing classes and then fail to carry over those skills to the history class; the department may consider whether the 101 course is trying to cover so much content that faculty don't have enough time to guide and give feedback about counter-argument.*

When faculty have enough information to feel comfortable acting, they may take one or more of these common types of action for gen ed courses:

- Faculty development. *For example, the department might decide to hold several brown bag lunches and evening meetings at various times (so adjuncts can attend), to share pedagogical strategies for helping students with counter-argument. The department might also post online resources for faculty.*

- Curricular change. *The department might decide to reduce the amount of material covered in History 101 and to ask that every instructor require an argumentative essay and work intensively with students on addressing counter-arguments. To help faculty with this task, the department might offer faculty development as above.*

- Collaboration. *Because the required first-year composition course teaches argument, the history department might talk with their writing program colleagues about how each addresses counter-arguments. The writing program might decide to emphasize counter-arguments more specifically and to include examples from history. The history faculty might agree that, as they teach students to address counter-arguments, they will specifically reference the composition class.*

The history department keeps two kinds of records of its deliberations:

1. *Minutes of its annual meeting for its own use in follow-up*
2. *A two-page report sent to the gen ed committee, summarizing:*
- *Time, date, and attendance at the meeting*
- *Data discussed; conclusions reached*
- *Item chosen for action*
- *Follow-up plans and actions*
- *Recommendations for items that need action at higher levels than the department*

Notice in this example that institution-wide surveys and standardized tests may augment and inform gen ed assessment within the department, but they do not replace it. The department is the most meaningful small unit in the institution. It controls money, appointments, and personnel decisions. It must take responsibility for the gen ed courses it offers. Unless it does, you will be trying to impose a superstructure of gen ed assessment that will always have to fight departmental apathy and disengagement. If the provost in the earlier example, with her disturbing national survey and standardized test results, had been working with departments that already were taking responsibility for assessing learning in their own general education courses, the provost could have fed her information into that departmental system, asking that departments, as they analyzed their students' work, pay particular attention to the areas that the national instruments had highlighted.

However, a system in which each isolated department only assesses its own general education courses will not suffice. You need a system for aggregating departmental results into an institution-wide view of student learning, and you need ways of using the aggregated data to take action at the institutional level.

Rewarding Departments for General Education Assessment

To provide incentive and reward for departments to assess their gen ed courses, you can use several strategies:

- *Leadership.* The institutional leaders emphasize and urge departments to assess gen ed courses. A chair orientation session is held to provide guidance. The chair supports gen ed assessment and institutes the annual meeting.
- *Ongoing system.* The members of the department are committed to gen ed assessment. The annual meeting is a regular part of their schedule; it takes place no matter who is the chair.
- *Assigned responsibility.* The assistant chair, or a specified faculty member, is charged with continuing oversight of the quality of the department's gen ed offerings, and assessment is part of that person's job.
- *Program review.* As part of its program review every seven years, the department is held responsible for gen ed assessment and for planning gen ed improvement. (More detail appears later in this section, and Chapter Two has more on program review.)
- *Gen ed course review.* Every five years, the department's gen ed courses come up for review by the gen ed committee. At that review, the department must show the committee that it is conducting assessment of its gen ed courses and using the assessment information for improvement. (More detail appears later in this section.)
- *Incentives.* The department is chosen as one of the "model" general education assessment departments. Each model department receives a financial award outside its normal budget; it agrees in turn to develop and disseminate its assessment system and to help other departments do the same.

You'll want to choose a combination of these motivating forces that works best for your institution.

Incorporating Assessment into Gen Ed Course Review

One of the motivational factors mentioned earlier is institutional review of general education courses. This means that all general education courses are reviewed, on a rotating schedule, to see whether they still meet general education goals and whether they are appropriately assessing student learning in the general education courses. Each department might have its general education offerings reviewed every five to seven years.

If you do not have a regular gen ed course review, you should institute it as soon as possible. I know all too many institutions that have a gazillion courses out there that count for gen ed credit, many of them accepted years ago, and nobody really knows what's going on in those courses or whether they are still serving the goals of gen ed. Students are simply set free with the instruction to take two courses in the humanities, two in natural sciences, and so on. The institution trusts that some kind of learning will take place, but it's very difficult to identify the learning these courses aim to foster, and even harder to determine whether the courses are fostering that learning. There's nothing intrinsically wrong with asking students to take two humanities courses and two science courses, but the faculty have to know why they believe this is an effective way to help students reach the institution's learning goals, and they have to assess whether in fact the students are achieving the goals.

If you are revising general education, you may have an opportunity to embed assessment from the beginning. Gaston and Gaff's *Revising General Education—And Avoiding the Potholes* (2009) is a practical guide to the process of general education revision, including but not limited to assessment. When gen ed is being revised, build in a five-year or seven-year review cycle.

But it's not enough just to conduct a review. The review has to include assessment. When a new course is being proposed for general education, or when current courses are being regularly reviewed for continued general education credit, it's common for the gen ed committee to ask for a syllabus and a set of learning objectives for the course, perhaps with an explicit discussion of how these learning objectives relate to the overall learning goals of gen ed. But that does not ensure that those goals are being assessed. For that, you'll need a document that specifically asks the department to describe how it assesses learning in its gen ed courses and how it uses assessment information for improvement. Exhibit 4.1 is an example of such a document written by a hypothetical department to the gen ed committee, for periodic review of the department's gen ed courses.

EXHIBIT 4.1

Sample Application from a Department for a General Education Course

Department: English

Course Title: Introduction to Literature

General Education Learning Goals Related to Course Objectives

General Education Learning Goals This Course Will Address	Course Objectives
Students will think critically and analytically about an issue, idea, or problem.	Students will write an essay using literary critical techniques to establish and defend an interpretation of literature, and will address counter-interpretations.
Students will communicate effectively orally and in writing to various audiences.	Students will express their ideas in discussion and written essays. The writing will be well-organized, clear, and consonant with Edited Standard Written English (ESWE).
Students will follow ethical principles for academic work.	Students will appropriately cite sources for their work. They will avoid plagiarism.
Students will demonstrate appreciation for cultures different from their own.	Students' interpretations of literature will demonstrate appreciation for the cultures and contexts from which the literature arises.

Question: How will student achievement of course objectives be measured?

Departmental Response:

- Each section of the course will require at least one literary-critical essay that will be evaluated by the instructor for each of the course objectives. (Individual faculty may devise more specific criteria or rubrics for specific assignments, as they choose. The department will provide sample rubrics and workshops on rubric use.)

- Annually, an outside researcher will conduct several focus groups of general education students from a range of general education sections, asking students how well they believed they achieved the learning goals, what aspects of the course most helped them learn, and what suggestions they have for improvement. The outsider will report the focus group results to the department, without identifying details about any individual faculty member. The report will focus on student feedback that can inform faculty development and department-level curricular or policy changes. The report will not be used for individual faculty members' personnel review.

Question: How will assessment information be used for classroom decision making? For departmental decision making?

Departmental Response:

- Classroom: Each faculty member will use his or her own classroom information for improvement.
- Annually, the general education instructors will meet in small groups to share their own plans for change and to recommend changes to the department as needed.
- The department will act as needed to address difficulties.
- The department will keep minutes of these meetings and records of its actions based on classroom assessment.

Question: If more than one faculty member is teaching the course, how does the department assure that all sections follow the guidelines explained above?

Departmental Response: Annually, the department distributes to all its gen ed faculty a copy of the objectives and guidelines for assessment. At the annual meeting, faculty share their findings about student strengths and weaknesses, and exchange ideas and best practices.

Question: Will the department be willing to submit an annual report to the general education committee reporting (in the aggregate) its faculty's findings about students' strengths and weaknesses, and its own actions?

Departmental Response: Yes

You will note that the department's proposal for its gen ed course asks that it be willing to submit periodic reports about its assessment. These reports can be two pages. They can ask three simple questions:

1. Measured against the gen ed learning goals, what are areas of difficulty for students in your department's gen ed courses? (The gen ed committee could specify a particular goal—say critical thinking or writing—to be addressed at a given point in time.)
2. How are you trying to address these areas? What has worked best?
3. What recommendations do you have for problems that need to be addressed at a level above the individual department?

It would not be difficult to read such two-page reports from each of thirty departments that offer gen ed courses and to identify

- Common areas in which many departments are noting difficulties
- Best practices for addressing the difficulties
- Areas that need attention at the institutional level

Incorporating Assessment into Departmental Program Review

The previous section suggested holding departments responsible for assessment by asking them periodically to submit their general education course proposals for review by the general education committee or a similar body. Another review process that may be used for general education is the department's program review. Institutions that have viable and useful systems of periodic program review for their departments sometimes bind review of the department's general education offerings into the larger program review. (Chapter Two discusses program review in more detail.)

The advantage of such a system is that the department can consider its gen ed needs as part of its total picture of planning and budgeting. Also, the system communicates to the department that general education is among its responsibilities. If the program review process is viable, departments often put considerable energy into it.

However, a drawback of binding gen ed assessment into program review is that, especially in research-intensive institutions, general education concerns may be lost as the review concentrates heavily on the department's standing in national research rankings or its ability to attract and place high-quality graduate students and majors. To address this problem, it may be helpful to have someone on the external or internal review committee who is specifically responsible for analyzing the department's assessment and improvement of its general education offerings and for ensuring that general education gets attention within the overall program review process.

Using Alternative Forums for Faculty Discussion

Sometimes departmental responsibility for general education assessment simply cannot be implemented effectively, at least not in a short time span. It may not be a propitious time to ask departments to take new forms of responsibility for general education. Or your program review system may be ineffective. If this is your situation, you should be positioning your institution to move toward increased departmental responsibility for general education, but in the meantime, you can find alternative forums in which to assess student learning in the distributive part of gen ed. Here are some suggestions:

- Organize assessment meetings not by department but by gen ed designation. For example, faculty whose gen ed courses are "writing intensive" could meet to consider data from W-I courses and take action. Faculty whose courses fulfill the "diversity" requirement could do the same. If faculty won't attend such meetings in sufficient numbers, work with a few representatives.

- Organize assessment meetings of subgroups of faculty within departments. For example, a writing program, a language program, or a required math course often have somewhat separate groups of faculty who teach and care about the gen ed courses. Could they gather to analyze data from their own courses and take action or make recommendations?

- If adjuncts teach significant portions of your gen ed courses, work with them. Hold meetings and retreats at which adjuncts examine data about student learning and recommend actions. Provide honoraria, meeting times that are convenient, and pleasant spaces where they can invest in student learning, where they feel they have a voice in institutional policy about gen ed, and where their efforts are visibly appreciated. Improvements arising from this group might include faculty development, online resources, or other forms of teaching support for adjuncts.

- Look for departments that *are* willing, and provide incentives. Are there a few departments that serve a substantial portion of the gen ed population and that would be willing to participate in departmental assessment if the department received extra resources for doing so?

In short, you're trying to find an effective forum for faculty discussion of data about student learning. Don't give up. Faculty are busy, and they are beset by forces that tug them toward concerns other than the gen ed program. But most faculty also care about learning, and they want to be responsible. You can build on that. And the adjuncts—gen ed is often the center of their attention, but they're underpaid, underappreciated, and tangential to the life of the institution. You could address that by paying, appreciating, and including them. So keep working to find a forum for discussion that will be effective for your faculty at your institution.

Using Institution-Wide Measures

Now we come to the bottom right-hand data boxes of Figure 4.1—the institution-wide measures. Chapter Two discusses in detail the decisions the institution might make about standardized tests, surveys, portfolios, and other data. The task of the general education director, committee, or other body charged with gen ed assessment and improvement is to incorporate the relevant aspects of these institution-wide instruments, along with information from departments or other faculty forums, into its processes of review and recommendation. Don't forget that national surveys often leave room for the institution to add a few questions, and these may be specific to your particular general education goals or issues.

Example: At one institution, the Institutional Research Office regularly sent out an invitation to departments and gen ed programs to propose extra questions for the student surveys and alumni surveys it administered. Institutional Research staff worked with the units to ensure that they constructed good questions, and that the blank slots were apportioned wisely among those who wanted to use them. The Office of Community-Based Learning used the extra slots periodically over more than a decade to gather a fine database of information about what students and alumni perceived they learned from their community-based learning, what aspects of the program they thought helped them, their suggestions for improvement, and (from data analysis by the Office of Institutional Research) correlations between students' survey responses and other factors such as their gender or major.

• • •

Example: At another institution, the National Survey of Student Engagement results showed that students at the institution wrote, revised, and used the writing center less frequently than students at peer institutions. The general education committee undertook its own survey of students and faculty in general education courses, attempting to verify the NSSE data and to get more detail about what was really going on. They chose an item for action.

Section Summary

- A basic no-frills general education assessment system relies for its basic measures on collection of student work and student surveys or focus groups within departments and programs. The information is used there for improvement and then passed on to be aggregated and used for decisions at higher levels.
- In my view, the most useful institution-wide measure is a student survey such as the NSSE or CCSSE. The NSSE Web site provides valuable ideas and case studies about how to use these instruments for improvement.

- You can conduct good general education assessment without standardized tests or institutional portfolios, provided you aggregate the data that departments have collected and use it for institutional action.
- Vehicles such as periodic review of gen ed courses, inclusion of gen ed in departmental program review, and other steps can provide incentives, rewards, and structures for departmental responsibility.

Reporting General Education Assessment

For reporting your general education assessment to audiences such as accreditors, you might collect the following:

- A diagram of your system, similar to Figure 4.1, but containing the specifics of your data and your committee and decision-making structures
- Prose to accompany the diagram, explaining how the system works
- A collection of documents that demonstrate how assessment works: for example, departmental proposals for new gen ed courses or for periodic review, showing how the departments assessed their general education offerings; minutes of one or two sample meetings where the general education committee or a similar body considered data about student learning and took or recommended action; or a written analysis of standardized test or survey scores that was actually presented to, and used by, a decision-making body
- Examples of actions taken on the basis of general education assessment data
- Analysis of strengths and weaknesses in your assessment system
- Plans for future improvements in the system

The information from these sources will be integrated with your assessment self-study, not only in the section about general education assessment, but in all your discussions about initiatives, programs, and policies that affect student learning. Chapter Two discusses in more detail how to report your assessment, and it offers an example of one institution's language for describing the assessment information that led to its general education reform.

Chapter Summary

- General education assessment can be made simple and manageable.
- Begin by reinforcing an overarching vision. Carefully define committee responsibilities. Adopt learning goals at both general and specific levels.
- Use the basic no-frills plan as a reference point.
- Departments need to take responsibility for assessing and improving their general education offerings. Use a variety of incentives and rewards.
- Standardized tests or portfolios can be effective if you use the information to inform action, but you do not need these measures to conduct good assessment of general education. You can collect student work and student reflections within departments, take action there, and then aggregate the information at higher levels for action.
- When accreditors or other audiences need to know how you're doing assessment, simply describe what you are doing, analyze it candidly, including its weaknesses, and share your plans for future improvement.

Appendix A

Curriculum Map

	Courses in Which the Learning Goals Are Addressed			
Learning Goals for Department, Program, or General Education	101	102	201	Additional Courses
Goal #1				
Goal #2				
Additional goals				

Instructors: For your course, place a "C" for every goal that your course covers but does not assess. You may mention this topic in class or assign readings about it, but you do not assess it in any major tests, exams, assignments, or projects.

Place an "A" next to any goal that your course both covers and assesses in a test, exam, assignment, or project.

Departments or programs: When instructors have completed the map for their own courses or sections, aggregate the results for findings about how various goals are addressed within the program as a whole.

Appendix B

Student Consent Form

Used for research reported in Walvoord (2008).

You are invited to participate in a study of teaching and learning in introductory courses in theology, religion, religious studies, biblical studies, or similar disciplines, nationwide. We hope to learn information about how teaching and learning take place in the class—information that will help future teachers of such courses to improve their teaching. The outcomes of the study may include such items as published articles, books, online resource materials for teachers, conference presentations, and workshop materials. Your teacher has accepted our invitation to be part of this study; now we are asking students in the class to agree that some of their work completed for the class may be used in the study.

The study will not take any extra time from you except what your teacher requires as part of the course. Your name will never be used in any outcome of this study. All your work will be anonymous. There are no known risks for you in this study. The rewards include an opportunity to benefit from your own self-reflection on your learning and to help future teachers of theology or religion.

If you agree to participate, some of your course material, including some of your papers or exams (all used without your name) will be sent by your teacher to the Principal Investigator and used in the study, along with similar material from students in the other fifty classes around the country. Three times during the semester, your teacher will ask you to reflect in writing, anonymously, during a few minutes of class time, about what aspects of the class are helping your learning, and what suggestions you have for changes. Your teacher will review these anonymous writings and will also share them with the Principal Investigator for the project. Finally, at the end of the course, you will complete an anonymous course evaluation, again addressing the effectiveness of the class for your learning, and your suggestions for change. These materials will be sent by your teacher to Prof. Barbara Walvoord, the Principal Investigator, at the University of Notre Dame, and will be included in the study along with similar material from about 2,000 students.

Your decision whether or not to participate will not affect in any way your future relations with your teacher or your institution. If you decide to participate, you are free to withdraw your consent and to discontinue participation at any time without penalty. If you have questions, please ask your teacher, or you may contact the project's Principal Investigator, Prof. Barbara E. Walvoord, Ph.D., Decio Hall 334, University of Notre Dame, Notre Dame, IN 46507. Phone 574-631-0101 or e-mail walvoord@nd.edu.

Please sign this form, submit one copy to your teacher, and keep the other copy for your records.

You are making a decision whether or not to participate. Your signature indicates that you are a student enrolled in this class and have decided to participate, having read the information provided above.

Please PRINT your name clearly _____

Signature: _____

Date: _____

Your Professor's Name _____

I am at least 18 years old _____yes   _____no

Appendix C

Analyzing Audiences for Assessment

Who?	Needs to Know What?	For What?
Institution or department	How well do our strategies for student learning work? What can we do to improve?	Make improvements
Institutional leaders and planners	What assessment strategies do we have in place? What do we need for successful assessment in the future?	Recommend changes for improvement of assessment Report to regional accreditor or other external audience
Accreditor	Does the institution meet our standards for an assessment system? What advice could we offer to help the institution improve its system?	Accreditation review
Prospective students	How good is this institution in helping me reach my learning, professional, and personal educational goals?	Enrollment
Donors	How well is this institution doing? Is it able to exercise appropriate accountability for my money?	Giving
Trustees, legislature	What assessment strategies are in place? What do we need to do to strengthen assessment? How well are the institution's students doing? Does the institution meet accreditation standards?	Funding, oversight, and interpreting the institution to various publics including businesses, voters, employers, and others

Appendix D
Sample Rubrics

The following two rubrics represent two different disciplines and two different ways of setting up a rubric: horizontal or vertical. Each rubric contains five levels of performance; rubrics may also have two, three, four, or even more levels. For more examples of rubrics and how to construct them, see Walvoord and Anderson, 2010.

Example 1: Rubric for Essay of Literary Analysis

Assignment: In an introduction to literature course, students wrote essays in which they advanced an interpretation of some aspect of the literary works they had been studying.

5	4	3	2	1
Thesis: The thesis of the paper is clear, complex, and challenging. It does not merely state the obvious or exactly repeat others' viewpoints, but it creatively and thoughtfully opens up our thinking about the work.	The thesis is both clear and reasonably complex.	The thesis of the paper is clear, though it may be unimaginative, largely a recapitulation of readings and class discussion, and/or fairly obvious.	Thesis is discernible, but the reader has to work to understand it, or the thesis seems to change as the essay proceeds.	Thesis is irrelevant to the assignment and/or not discernible.
Complexity and Originality: The essay is unusually thoughtful, deep, creative, and far-reaching in its analysis. The writer explores the subject from various points of view, acknowledges alternative interpretations and varied literary critical lenses, and recognizes the complexity of issues in literature and in life. Other works we have read and ideas we have discussed are integrated as relevant. The essay shows a curious mind at work.	The essay is thoughtful and extensive in its analysis. It acknowledges alternative interpretations and recognizes complexity in literature and in life. Some other works are integrated as relevant.	The writer goes somewhat beyond merely paraphrasing someone else's point of view or repeating what was discussed in class AND/OR the essay does not integrate other relevant works we have read.	Writer moves only marginally beyond merely paraphrasing someone else's point of view or repeating what was discussed in class.	The paper is mere paraphrase or repetition of class discussion.

(continued)

	5	4	3	2	1
Organization and Coherence:	The reader feels that the writer is in control of the direction and organization of the essay. The essay follows a logical line of reasoning to support its thesis and to deal with counter-evidence and alternative viewpoints. Subpoints are fashioned so as to open up the topic in the most effective way.	As for 5 but subpoints may not be fashioned to open up the topic in the most effective way.	The reader feels that the writer is in control of the direction and organization of the essay most of the time. The essay generally follows a logical line of reasoning to support its thesis.	The essay has some discernible main points.	The essay has no discernible plan of organization.
Evidence, Support:	The writer's claims and interpretations are backed with evidence from the literature, works we have read, secondary sources, and sensible reasoning. The writer assumes the reader has read the work and does not need the plot repeated, but the writer refers richly and often to the events and words of the literary works to support his/her points.	As for 5 but the writer may occasionally drop into mere plot summary.	The writer's claims and interpretations about the works are generally backed with at least some evidence from the works AND/OR the writer includes significant passages that are mere plot summary.	The writer's claims are only sometimes backed with evidence AND/OR large sections of the paper are mere plot summary.	The paper is primarily plot summary.
Voice and Tone:	The language is clear, precise, and elegant. It achieves a scholarly tone without sounding pompous. It is the authentic voice of a curious mind at work, talking to other readers of the literary work.	The language is clear and precise.	The language is understandable throughout.	The language is sometimes confusing. Several sentences do not track.	The language is often confusing. Sentences and paragraphs do not track.
Sources:	The essay integrates secondary sources smoothly. It quotes when the exact words of another author are important, and otherwise paraphrases. It does not just string together secondary sources, but uses them to support the writer's own thinking. Each source is identified in the text, with some statement about its author; there are no quotes just stuck into the text without explanation.	As for 5 but sources may be quoted with no contextual explanation AND/OR writer uses direct quotation when paraphrase would be better, or vice versa.	The essay incorporates some secondary sources and connects them to the writer's own points.	The essay strings together secondary sources with little or no explicit connection to the writer's own points.	There is no use of secondary sources.

Grammar, Punctuation, Sentence Effectiveness: There are no discernible departures from Standard Edited Written English (ESWE). The sentences are easily readable; their meaning is clear. Words are precise, relationships among sentence parts are clear, parallel forms are used for parallel ideas, and sentence structure and length are used for rhetorical purposes.	There are a few departures from ESWE AND/OR the sentences are generally clear and readable, but some words may be poorly chosen; some sentences may not make relations clear.	There are no more than an average of two departures from ESWE per page in the critical areas listed below. The sentences are usually clear.	There are more than two departures from ESWE. A few sentences may be unclear.	Many departures from ESWE and poorly constructed sentences interfere with meaning.

Critical Areas:

- Spelling or typos
- Sentence boundary punctuation (run-ons, comma splices, fused sentences, fragments)
- Use of apostrophe, -s, and -es
- Pronoun forms
- Pronoun agreement, and providing antecedents for pronouns
- Verb forms and subject-verb agreement
- Use of gender-neutral language
- Capitalization of proper nouns and of first words in the sentence

Example 2: Rubric for Scientific Experiment in Biology Capstone Course

By Virginia Johnson Anderson, Towson University, Towson, Maryland

Assignment: Semester-long assignment to design an original experiment, carry it out, and write it up in scientific report format. This is the major assignment in this course, titled "Scientific Research." The course was instituted recently as a result of employer feedback that students were insufficiently prepared to really understand and carry out the scientific method. The goal of the course is to prepare students to conduct original scientific research and present it orally and in writing. There were no resources to make this a lab course, so the students had to conduct research outside the lab. Many student graduates will be working with commercial products in commercial labs in the area, e.g., Noxell. In the assignment, students are to determine which of two brands of a commercial product (e.g., two brands of popcorn) is "best." They must base their judgment on at least four experimental factors (e.g., "percentage of kernels popped" is an experimental factor; price is not, because it is written on the package).

Title

5 Is appropriate in tone and structure to science journal; contains necessary descriptors, brand names, and allows reader to anticipate design.

4 Is appropriate in tone and structure to science journal; most descriptors present; identifies function of experimentation, suggests design, but lacks brand names.

3 Identifies function, brand name, but does not allow reader to anticipate design.

2 Identifies function or brand name, but not both; lacks design information or is misleading

1 Is patterned after another discipline or missing.

Introduction

5 Clearly identifies the purpose of the research; identifies interested audiences; adopts an appropriate tone.

4 Clearly identifies the purpose of the research; identifies interested audiences.

3 Clearly identifies the purpose of the research.

2 Purpose present in Introduction, but must be identified by reader.

1 Fails to identify the purpose of the research.

Scientific Format Demands

5   All material placed in the correct sections; organized logically within each section; runs parallel among different sections.

4   All material placed in correct sections; organized logically within sections, but may lack parallelism among sections.

3   Material placed in proper sections but not well organized within the sections; disregards parallelism.

2   Some materials are placed in the wrong sections or are not adequately organized wherever they are placed.

1   Material placed in wrong sections or not sectioned; poorly organized wherever placed.

Materials and Methods Section

5   Contains effective, quantifiable, concisely organized information that allows the experiment to be replicated; is written so that all information inherent to the document can be related back to this section; identifies sources of all data to be collected; identifies sequential information in an appropriate chronology; does not contain unnecessary, wordy descriptions of procedures.

4   As in 5, but contains unnecessary information, and/or wordy descriptions within the section.

3   Presents an experiment that is definitely replicable; all information in document may be related to this section; but fails to identify some sources of data and/or presents sequential information in a disorganized, difficult way.

2   Presents an experiment that is marginally replicable; parts of the basic design must be inferred by the reader; procedures not quantitatively described; some information in Results or Conclusions cannot be anticipated by reading the Materials and Methods section.

1   Describes the experiment so poorly or in such a nonscientific way that it cannot be replicated.

Nonexperimental Information

5   Student researches and includes price and other nonexperimental information that would be expected to be significant to the audience in determining the better product, or specifically states nonexperimental factors excluded by design; interjects these at appropriate positions in text or develops a weighted rating scale; integrates nonexperimental information in the Conclusions.

4   As in 5, but is less effective in developing the significance of the nonexperimental information.

3   Student introduces price and other nonexperimental information, but does not integrate them into Conclusions.

2   Student researches and includes price effectively; does not include or specifically exclude other nonexperimental information.

1   Student considers price and other nonexperimental variables as research variables; fails to identify the significance of these factors to the research.

Experimental Design

5   Student selects experimental factors that are appropriate to the research purpose and audience; measures adequate aspects of these selected factors; establishes discrete subgroups for which data significance may vary; student demonstrates an ability to eliminate bias from the design and bias-ridden statements from the research; student selects appropriate sample size, equivalent groups, and statistics; student designs a superior experiment.

4   As in 5, but student designs an adequate experiment.

3   Student selects experimental factors that are appropriate to the research purpose and audience; measures adequate aspects of these selected factors; establishes discrete subgroups for which data significance may vary; research is weakened by bias *or* by sample size of less than 10.

2   As in 3, but research is weakened by bias *and* inappropriate sample size.

1   Student designs a poor experiment.

Operational Definitions

5   Student constructs a stated comprehensive operational definition and well-developed specific operational definitions.

4   Student constructs an implied comprehensive operational definition and well-developed specific operational definitions.

3   Student constructs an implied (though possibly less clear) comprehensive operational definition and some specific operational definitions.

2   Student constructs specific operational definitions but fails to construct a comprehensive definition.

1   Student lacks understanding of operational definition.

Control of Variables

5 Student demonstrates, by written statement, the ability to control variables by experimental control and by randomization; student makes reference to, or implies, factors to be disregarded by reference to pilot or experience; superior overall control of variables.

4 As in 5, but student demonstrates an adequate control of variables.

3 Student demonstrates the ability to control important variables experimentally; Materials and Methods section does not indicate knowledge of randomization or selectively disregards variables.

2 Student demonstrates the ability to control some, but not all, of the important variables experimentally.

1 Student demonstrates a lack of understanding about controlling variables.

Collecting Data and Communicating Results

5 Student selects quantifiable experimental factors and defines and establishes quantitative units of comparison; measures the quantifiable factors and units in appropriate quantities or intervals; student selects appropriate statistical information to be utilized in the results; when effective, student displays results in graphs with correctly labeled axes; data are presented to the reader in text as well as graphic forms; tables or graphs have self-contained headings.

4 As in 5, but the student did not prepare self-contained headings for tables or graphs.

3 As in 4, but data reported in graphs or tables contain materials that are irrelevant or not statistically appropriate.

2 Student selects quantifiable experimental factors or defines and establishes quantitative units of comparison; fails to select appropriate quantities or intervals or fails to display information graphically when appropriate.

1 Student does not select, collect, or communicate quantifiable results.

Interpreting Data

5 Student summarizes the purpose and findings of the research; student draws inferences that are consistent with the data and scientific reasoning and relates these to interested audiences; student explains expected results and offers explanations or suggestions for further research for unexpected results; student presents data honestly, distinguishes

between fact and implication, and avoids overgeneralizing; student organizes nonexperimental information to support conclusion; student accepts or rejects the hypothesis.

4   As in 5, but student does not accept or reject the hypothesis.

3   As in 4, but the student overgeneralizes or fails to organize non-experimental information to support conclusions.

2   Student summarizes the purpose and findings of the research; student explains expected results but ignores unexpected results.

1   Student may or may not summarize the results but fails to interpret their significance to interested audiences.

Source: Adapted from Anderson and Walvoord, 1990, Appendix A. Copyright 2007 by the National Council of Teachers of English. Used with permission.

Resources

A Short List

If I were to select just a few resources to augment this one, I would choose the following:

Banta, T. W., Jones, E. A., and Black, K. E. *Designing Effective Assessment: Principles and Profiles of Good Practice*. San Francisco: Jossey-Bass, 2009. Case studies combined with principles extracted from those studies, by preeminent experts in the field.

Kuh, G. D., Kinzie, J., Buckley, J. A., Bridges, B. K., and Hayek, J. C. *Piecing Together the Student Success Puzzle: Research, Propositions, and Recommendations*. ASHE Higher Education Report: Vol. 32, no. 5. San Francisco: Jossey-Bass, 2007. Sensible, useable, and well-informed summary of research on what really matters to student success.

National Survey of Student Engagement (NSSE). *Using NSSE to Assess and Improve Undergraduate Education: Lessons from the Field 2009*. Bloomington, IN: National Survey of Student Engagement, 2009. How to use survey results (and by implication, other assessment data) for improvement of student learning.

Suskie, L. *Assessing Student Learning: A Common Sense Guide* (2nd ed.). San Francisco: Jossey-Bass, 2009. Twice as long as this book. A sensible and comprehensive guide by an experienced leader in the field.

Walvoord, B. E., and Anderson, V. J. *Effective Grading: A Tool for Learning and Assessment in College* (2nd ed.). San Francisco: Jossey-Bass, 2010. A guide for the classroom instructor to grading and its contexts, including making assignments, communicating with students, and guiding the learning process. Final sections discuss how to use student classroom work for assessment in one's own classroom, in grant-funded projects, in departments, general education, and the institution.

References

Alberts, Scott. [salberts@truman.edu]. "Publication About Truman State." Private e-mail message to Barbara Walvoord [walvoord@nd.edu]. July 31, 2009.

Anderson, V. J., and Walvoord, B. E. "Conducting and Reporting Original Scientific Research: Anderson's Biology Class." In B. E. Walvoord and L. P. McCarthy, *Thinking and Writing in College: A Naturalistic Study of Students in Four Disciplines.* Urbana, IL: National Council of Teachers of English, 1990.

Association of American Colleges and Universities. "Academic Freedom and Educational Responsibility: AAC&U Board of Directors' Statement, January 6, 2006." [www.aacu.org/about/statement/academic_freedom.cfm].

Banta, T. W. (ed.). *Community College Assessment: Assessment Update Collections.* San Francisco: Jossey-Bass, 2004.

Banta, T. W. "Reliving the History of Large-Scale Assessment in Higher Education." *Assessment Update*, 2006, *18*(4). Report in T. W. Banta (ed.), *Assessing Student Achievement in General Education.* San Francisco: Jossey-Bass, 2007.

Banta, T. W. (ed.). *Assessing Student Learning in the Disciplines: Assessment Update Collections.* San Francisco: Jossey-Bass, 2007a.

Banta, T. W. (ed.). *Assessing Student Achievement in General Education.* San Francisco: Jossey-Bass, 2007b.

Banta, T. W. "Introduction: Assessing Student Achievement in General Education." In T. W. Banta (ed.), *Assessing Student Achievement in General Education.* San Francisco: Jossey-Bass, 2007c.

Banta, T. W., and Associates (eds.). *Portfolio Assessment Uses, Cases, Scoring, and Impact: Assessment Update Collections.* San Francisco: Jossey-Bass, 2003.

Banta, T. W., Jones, E. A., and Black, K. E. *Designing Effective Assessment: Principles and Profiles of Good Practice.* San Francisco: Jossey-Bass, 2009.

Banta, T. W., and Pike, G. R. "Revisiting the Blind Alley of Value Added." *Assessment Update*, 2007, *19*(1), 1–2, 14–15.

Bergquist, W. H., and Pawlak, K. *Engaging the Six Cultures of the Academy: Revised and Expanded Edition of The Four Cultures of the Academy.* (2nd ed.) San Francisco: Jossey-Bass, 2008.

Brainard, J. "When Is Research Really Research?" *Chronicle of Higher Education*, Nov. 26, 2004, p. A21.

Braskamp, L. A., Trautvetter, L. C., and Ward, K. *Putting Students First: How Colleges Develop Students Purposefully.* Bolton, MA: Anker, 2006.

Bresciani, M. J. (ed.). *Assessing Student Learning in General Education: Good Practice Case Studies.* Bolton, MA: Anker, 2007.

Bresciani, M. J. *Outcomes-Based Academic and Co-Curricular Program Review.* Sterling, VA: Stylus, 2006.

Cambridge, B. (ed.). *Electronic Portfolios: Emerging Practices in Students, Faculty, and Institutional Learning.* Washington, DC: American Association for Higher Education, 2001.

Cameron, J. A. "Living Rubrics: Sustaining Collective Reflection, Deliberation, and Revision of Program Outcomes." In T. W. Banta, E. A. Jones, and K. E. Black, *Designing Effective Assessment: Principles and Profiles of Good Practice.* San Francisco: Jossey-Bass, 2009.

Choban, M. D., Choban, G. M., and Choban, D. "Strategic Planning and Decision Making in Higher Education: What Gets Attention and What Doesn't." *Assessment Update,* 2008, *20*(2), 1–2, 13–14.

Chickering, A. W., and Gamson, Z. F. "Seven Principles for Good Practice in Undergraduate Education." *AAHE Bulletin,* 1987, *39*(7), 3–7.

Erwin, T. D. "Standardized Testing and Accountability." In J. C. Burke and Associates (eds.), *Achieving Accountability in Higher Education: Balancing Public, Academic, and Market Demands.* San Francisco: Jossey-Bass, 2004.

Ewell, P. T. "Can Assessment Serve Accountability? It Depends on the Question." In J. C. Burke and Associates (eds.), *Achieving Accountability in Higher Education: Balancing Public, Academic, and Market Demands.* San Francisco: Jossey-Bass, 2004.

Ewell, P. T. "Power in Numbers: The Values in Our Metrics." *Change,* 2005, *37*(4), 10–16.

Ewell, P. T. *U.S. Accreditation and the Future of Quality Assurance: A Tenth Anniversary Report from the Council for Higher Education Accreditation.* Boulder, CO: National Center for Higher Education Management Systems, 2008.

Forest, J.J.F. and Keith, B. "Assessing Students' Moral Awareness." *Assessment Update,* 2004, *16*(1). Report in T. W. Banta (ed.), *Assessing Student Achievement in General Education.* San Francisco: Jossey-Bass, 2007.

Gaston, P. L., and Gaff, J. C. *Revising General Education—And Avoiding the Potholes.* Washington, DC: Association of American Colleges and Universities, 2009.

Gelmon, S. B., Holland, B. A., Driscoll, A., Spring, A., and Kerrigan, S. *Assessing Service Learning and Civic Engagement: Principles and Techniques.* Providence: Brown University, Campus Compact, 2001.

Hunt, S. "Community College Strategies: Using a Capstone Course to Assess General Education Outcomes." *Assessment Update,* 2000, *12*(2). Report in T. Banta (ed.),

Assessing Student Achievement in General Education: Assessment Update Collections. San Francisco: Jossey-Bass, 2007.

Jacobs, D. C. "A Chemical Mixture of Methods." In P. Hutchings (ed.), *Opening Lines: Approaches to the Scholarship of Teaching and Learning.* Menlo Park, CA: Carnegie Foundation for the Advancement of Teaching, 2000.

Kuh, G. D. *High-Impact Educational Practices: What They Are, Who Has Access to Them, and Why They Matter.* Washington, DC: Association of American Colleges and Universities, 2008.

Kuh, G. D., and Hinkle, S. E. "Enhancing Student Learning through Collaboration Between Academic Affairs and Student Affairs." In R. M. Diamond (ed.), *A Field Guide for Academic Leaders.* San Francisco: Jossey-Bass, 2002.

Kuh, G. D., Kinzie, J., Buckley, J. A., Bridges, B. K., and Hayek, J. C. *Piecing Together the Student Success Puzzle: Research, Propositions, and Recommendations.* ASHE Higher Education Report: Volume 32, no. 5. San Francisco: Jossey-Bass, 2007.

Kuh, G. D., Kinzie, J., Schuh, J. H., Whitt, E. J., and Associates. *Student Success in College: Creating Conditions That Matter.* San Francisco: Jossey-Bass, 2005a.

Kuh, G. D., Kinzie, J., Schuh, J. H., and Whitt, E. J. *Assessing Conditions to Enhance Educational Effectiveness: The Inventory for Student Engagement and Success.* San Francisco: Jossey-Bass, 2005b.

Maki, P. L. *Assessing for Learning: Building a Sustainable Commitment Across the Institution.* Sterling, VA: Stylus, 2004. Copyright by the American Association for Higher Education.

National Survey of Student Engagement (NSSE). *Using NSSE to Assess and Improve Undergraduate Education: Lessons from the Field 2009.* Bloomington, IN: National Survey of Student Engagement, 2009.

New England Association of Schools and Colleges (NEASC). *Standards for Accreditation.* [http://www.cihe.neasc.org]. 2005.

Palomba, C. A., and Banta, T. W. (eds.). *Assessing Student Competence in Accredited Disciplines: Pioneering Approaches to Assessment in Higher Education.* Sterling, VA: Stylus, 2001.

Pascarella, E. T., and Terenzini, P. T. *How College Affects Students: A Third Decade of Research.* San Francisco: Jossey-Bass, 2005.

Pike, G. R. "Assessment Measures: Value-Added Models and the Collegiate Learning Assessment." *Assessment Update*, 2006, *18*(4), 5–7.

Pike, G. R. "Assessment Measures: Making Accountability Transparent: Next Steps for the Voluntary System of Accountability." *Assessment Update*, 2008, *20*(2), 8–9, 12.

Reynolds, C. "Santa Fe Community College and the CCSSE: Using Data to Make Meaningful Change." *Assessment Update*, 2007, *19*(5), 4–6.

Schroeder, C. C., Minor, F. D., and Tarkow, T. A. "Freshman Interest Groups: Partnership for Promoting Student Success." *New Directions for Student Services,* Vol. 87. San Francisco: Jossey-Bass, 1999.

Serban, A. M., and Friedlander, J. *Developing and Implementing Assessment of Student Learning Outcomes.* New Directions for Community Colleges, no. 126. San Francisco: Jossey-Bass, 2004.

Seybert, J. A., and O'Hara, K. A. "Development of a Performance-Based Model for Assessment of General Education." *Assessment Update,* 1997, *9*(4), 5–7.

Shavelson, R. J. "Assessing Student Learning Responsibly: From History to Audacious Proposal." *Change,* 2007, *39*(1), 26–33.

Shermis, M. D. "The Collegiate Learning Assessment: A Critical Perspective." *Assessment Update,* 2008, *20*(2), 10–12.

Shulman, L. S. 2007. "Counting and Re-counting: Assessment and the Quest for Accountability." *Change,* 2007, *39*(1), 20–25.

Stevens, D. D., and Levi, A. J. *Introduction to Rubrics.* Sterling, VA: Stylus, 2005.

Suskie, L. *Assessing Student Learning: A Common Sense Guide.* (2nd ed.) San Francisco: Jossey-Bass, 2009.

Tobias, S. *Revitalizing Undergraduate Science: Why Some Things Work and Most Don't.* Tucson: Research Corp., 1992.

U.S. Department of Health and Human Services. Title 45, Part 46, "Protection of Human Subjects." Section 101, "To What Does This Policy Apply?" 2008. [www.gpoaccess.gov/cfr/index.html]. Choose "How to Link to CFR Documents." Fill in Title 45, Part 46, Section 101 and click "generate." Downloaded July 21, 2009.

Walvoord, B. E. *Teaching and Learning in College Introductory Religion Courses.* Malden, MA: Blackwell, 2008.

Walvoord, B. E., and Anderson, V. J. *Effective Grading: A Tool for Learning and Assessment in College.* (2nd ed.) San Francisco: Jossey-Bass, 2010.

Walvoord, B. E., Carey, A. K., Smith, H. L., Soled, S. W., Way, P. K., and Zorn, D. *Academic Departments: How They Work, How They Change.* ASHE-ERIC Higher Education Report Vol. 27, no. 8. San Francisco: Jossey-Bass, 2000.

Womack, N. H. "Isothermal Community College: General Education Case Study." In M. J. Bresciani (ed.), *Assessing Student Learning in General Education: Good Practice Case Studies.* Bolton, MA: Anker, 2007.

Zubizarreta, J. *The Learning Portfolio: Reflective Practice for Improving Student Learning.* (2nd ed.) San Francisco: Jossey-Bass, 2009.

Index